T5-BYK-695

Rethinking
Children's Play

Companion Website Available

The Companion Website relating to this book is available online at:
http://education.brown.continuumbooks.com

Please visit the link and register with us to receive your password
and access to the Companion Website.

If you experience any problems accessing the Companion Website,
please contact Bloomsbury at info@continuumbooks.com

Also available in the *New Childhoods* Series

Rethinking Childhood, Phil Jones

Rethinking Children and Families, Nick Frost

Rethinking Children and Research, Mary Kellett

Rethinking Children's Rights, Sue Welch and Phil Jones

Rethinking Children, Violence and Safeguarding, Lorraine Radford

Also available from Bloomsbury

Playing Outdoors in the Early Years, Ros Garrick

Rethinking
Children's Play

Fraser Brown and Michael Patte

New Childhoods Series

B L O O M S B U R Y

LONDON • NEW DELHI • NEW YORK • SYDNEY

HUMBER LIBRARIES LAKESHORE CAMPUS
3199 Lakeshore Blvd West
TORONTO, ON.   M8V 1K8

Bloomsbury Academic

An imprint of Bloomsbury Publishing Plc

50 Bedford Square	175 Fifth Avenue
London	New York
WC1B 3DP	NY 10010
UK	USA

www.bloomsbury.com

First published 2013

© Fraser Brown and Michael Patte, 2013

All rights reserved. No part of this publication may be reproduced or transmitted in any form or by any means, electronic or mechanical, including photocopying, recording, or any information storage or retrieval system, without prior permission in writing from the publishers.

Fraser Brown and Michael Patte have asserted their right under the Copyright, Designs and Patents Act, 1988, to be identified as Authors of this work.

No responsibility for loss caused to any individual or organization acting on or refraining from action as a result of the material in this publication can be accepted by Bloomsbury Academic or the author.

British Library Cataloguing-in-Publication Data
A catalogue record for this book is available from the British Library.

ISBN: HB: 978-1-4411-7366-9
PB: 978-1-4411-9469-5

Library of Congress Cataloging-in-Publication Data
A catalog record for this book is available from the Library of Congress

Typeset by Fakenham Prepress Solutions, Fakenham, Norfolk, NR21 8NN
Printed and bound in Great Britain

Contents

Introduction to the New Childhoods Series

The amount of current attention given to children and to childhood is unprecedented. Recent years have seen the agreement of new international conventions, national bodies established, and waves of regional and local initiatives all concerning children.

This rapid pace has been set by many things. Demand from children themselves, from adults working with children, from governments and global bodies, new ideas and raw needs: all are fuelling change. Within and, often, leading the movement is research. From the work of multinational corporations designed to reach into the minds of children and the pockets of parents, through to charity-driven initiatives aiming to challenge the forces that situate children in extreme poverty, a massive amount of energy is expended in research relating to children and their lives. Research can be seen as original investigation undertaken in order to gain knowledge and understanding through a systematic and rigorous process of critical enquiry examining "even the most commonplace assumption" (Kellett 2005, p. 9). This attention is not all benign. As Kellett has pointed out, the findings can be used by the media to saturate and accost, rather than support under-12s who are seen as "obese", for example, or to stigmatize young people by the use of statistics. However, research can also play a role in investigating, enquiring, communicating and understanding for the benefit of children and young people. Recent years have seen innovations in the focus of research, as political moves that challenge the ways in which children have been silenced and excluded result in previously unseen pictures of children's experiences of poverty, family life or community. The attitudes, opinions and lived experiences of children are being given air, and one of the themes within the "New Childhoods" series concerns the opportunities and challenges this is creating. As this book will reveal, research is being used to set new agendas, to challenge ways of living and working that oppress, harm or limit children. It is also being used to test preconceptions and long-held beliefs about children's lived experiences. In addition to the focus of research, innovations are being made in the way research is conceived and carried out. Its role in children's lives is changing. In the past much research treated children as objects; research was done on them, with the agenda and framework set purely by adults. New work is emerging where children create the way in which research is conceived and carried out. Children act as researchers, and researchers work with questions formulated by children or work with children.

This series aims to offer access to some of the challenges, discoveries and work-in-progress of contemporary research. The terms *child* and *childhood* are used within the series in line with Article 1 of the United Nations Convention on the Rights of the Child which defines "children" as persons up to the age of 18. The books offer opportunities to engage with emerging ideas, questions and practices. They will help those studying childhood, or living and working with children to become familiar with challenging work, to engage with findings and to reflect on their own ideas, experiences and ways of working.

Phil Jones, Institute of Education, University of London, UK

Acknowledgements

The authors would like to acknowledge the support of their families and friends, who have shown immense patience and understanding during the writing of this book. We would also like to acknowledge the contributions of close colleagues and students, too numerous to mention. We are immensely grateful for their valuable suggestions and thoughtful advice. In particular we should mention the tireless support of the series editor Phil Jones. He has been patience personified.

Royalties

All royalties from the sale of this book will go to Aid for Romanian Children, whose work is mentioned in several chapters of the book. The charity works with children in Romania to relieve poverty and hardship; alleviate sickness and distress; and advance development through play and education (see: www.arccharity.org)

Introduction

Introduction and key questions

Worries about the disappearance of play in the lives of children are not a recent phenomenon. Such fears were prevalent in the early 1960s and prompted the creation of the International Play Association (IPA) in Denmark to promote, protect, and preserve play as a basic human right for all children. Since then a number of non-governmental organizations and non-profit foundations have sprouted up around the world to advocate for the value of play, and to speak out over concerns of its marginalization. These include the National Institute for Play and the Alliance for Childhood in America, the Fair Play for Children Campaign in the UK, and The Association for the Study of Play (a world-wide organization). Even with such groups advocating for play to enrich the daily lives of children, various cultural dynamics dictate that many children in the developed world experience daily schedules that would not be tolerated by adults. Such a stance marginalizes the necessity of play throughout childhood.

In the past children were often viewed as "miniature adults" (Postman 1982, p.41), but such conceptions of childhood have become outdated with time, due in large part to the gradual realization that children need ample time to grow and develop. This precious time serves as a vital transition between infancy and adulthood. Proponents embracing the sacredness of childhood recognize the importance of including ample time for play, coupled with freedom to explore the natural environment. The key question that emerges is this: in a society where play has shifted from its previously unstructured child-initiated focus to a more structured educational concept, bent on early academic preparation, whether we intend to preserve our sense that childhood is inextricably interwoven with the concept of free play.

This book is organized into three parts, with part one providing the reader with a foundation and background of play theory (Chapter 1). Part two of the book explores how play is actualized throughout society today and identifies a variety of societal factors devaluing play (Chapters 2, 3 and 4). The reader is also asked to consider the extreme consequences of play's marginalization for children and society through an examination of play deprivation (Chapter 5). Part three offers solutions for addressing the forces working against play identified throughout the text. This part also offers some provocations for the reader to consider (Chapters 6 and 7).

The format of each chapter is structured to be accessible for the reader through offering current and classical theory on play, summaries of recent and relevant play research, and a combination of intellectual and practical activities that allow for the application of play theory and the deeper exploration of the research.

Some of the activities invite the reader to undertake their own observations of children's play. In some cases this may raise interesting and challenging issues in terms of ethics; for example, readers may have to consider issues of anonymity, confidentiality, informed consent and the right to withdraw (see Alderson 1995 or Farrell 2005 for a discussion of these issues). If the reader has access within their professional world to children playing, then it may be possible to draw on this in their exploration of the activities. In some cases an alternative activity is offered for those who do not have such access, usually inviting the reader to reflect on a specific research example. It may sometimes be possible to negotiate suitable access, but the reader would almost certainly have to satisfy the security requirements that apply in their own country; for example, in the UK they would have to acquire a satisfactory Criminal Records Bureau check (Home Office 2012).

The book attempts to address the following questions.

- What is play?
- What opportunities exist for play in society at the moment?
- How are those opportunities being eroded?
- What happens when play is restricted?
- What are the possible solutions?
- Can play be a mechanism for addressing social ills?

What is play?

A hard and true fact about play is that it is easy to recognize but difficult to define. Theorists throughout history have offered myriad definitions, views, and theories about play. Many classic and contemporary scholars (Dewey 1916; Bredekamp & Rosegrant 1995) distinguish play from what they view as its binary opposite work. Viewed through this lens play is thought to be frivolous and most popular during the years of childhood whereas work that is viewed as more serious in nature happens most frequently during the years of adulthood.

What opportunities exist for play in society at the moment?

Play has been a constant element in the lives of children for generations. Engaging in various forms of play provided countless opportunities for children to experience various colors, sights, and sounds that etched vivid memories and impressions. These experiences stimulated the senses, invigorated the spirit, and enlivened the soul (Patte 2010). However, for many children today, play reflects a dramatic shift from its previous child-initiated basis of unstructured play to one endorsing an educational focus for early academic preparation. Through this prism, opportunities to engage in self-directed, spontaneous play are no more than a distant memory. To highlight, Miller and Almon (2009) found that kindergarten has changed radically in the past twenty years and that "children today spend far more time being taught and assessed on literacy and math skills than they do learning through play and exploration, exercising their bodies and using their imaginations" (p.11). Just thirty years ago, 40 per cent of a typical school day was devoted to child-initiated play, compared to 25 per cent today (Miller & Almon 2009).

How are those opportunities being eroded?

There are many logistical and psychological barriers that impede opportunities for children to engage in various forms of play. These barriers include
fear, access to quality play spaces, increased amounts of screen time, and a
reduction in school-based playtime. Fear serves as a major barrier impeding
play opportunities and according to both Elkind (2007) and Gill (2007), that
fear causes parents to overinvest, overprotect, and over-programme the lives
of their children. Gaining access to quality play spaces is a second barrier
impacting opportunities for children to play (Colabianchi et al. 2009). In a
recent poll, 59 per cent of parents reported that there was no outdoor play
space within walking distance from their home; in lower socioeconomic
neighbourhoods, the number jumped to 69 per cent (KaBOOM 2009). The
prevalence of technology in the lives of children makes screen time an
additional barrier affecting time for their play. Screen time in a variety of forms
has all but replaced more active and creative play opportunities for children.
The elimination and reduction of recess and play in school is a final barrier
that speaks to the diminished value of play throughout society. To highlight,
over 40,000 schools throughout America no longer have recess and those that
do average between 15–20 minutes per day (Marano 2008; Patte 2009).

What happens when play is restricted?

There is mounting evidence across multiple disciplines that links dimin-
ishing amounts of time to engage in various forms of play to negative
outcomes for children. These negative outcomes include impaired social
competence (National Association of Early Childhood Specialists in State
Departments of Education 2002); increased incidence of Attention Deficit
Hyperactive Disorder (Marano 2008); child fragility (Marano 2008); the
childhood obesity epidemic (Ogden et al. 2010); increased incidence of
anxiety and depression (Panksepp 2002); a decrease in creativity and imagination (Marano 2008); inflexibility (Bekoff & Pierce 2009); and adversity to
risk (Gill 2007; Marano 2008).

What are the possible solutions?

In the book *Playwork: theory and practice* playwork was described as "a
mechanism for redressing aspects of developmental imbalance caused by
a deficit of play opportunities" (2003a, p.52). It follows, therefore, that the

playwork approach is well suited to address the societal factors devaluing children's play in our modern society. However, the practical application of the playwork approach should be handled with caution. It would be misguided to think that playworkers view play solely as part of the child's preparation for adulthood, or that their role is merely something Sturrock called "adult-generated corrective adjustment" (2007, p.iii). Playwork is not about adults taking control of children's lives; quite the opposite. Playworkers see children as "the subjects of their own development," and play as a process of both "being and becoming" (ibid). It is only during play that children are likely to experience being in control of their own destiny. In practice, playwork is substantially about creating environments that enable children to play freely. The most effective playwork environment, therefore, has little intervention from the playworker once the basic parameters have been set. Put simply, the role of the playworker is to provide the setting, the tools, and the materials, and leave the rest to the children, albeit having regard for their safety and security. In the words of John Portchmouth, "It helps if someone no matter how lightly puts in our way the means of making use of what we find" (1969, p.7).

Can play be a mechanism for addressing social ills?

Brown (2008) found that children's learning and development derive substantially from the creation of an enriched play environment that is supportive of the play process. The use of negative capability, the suspension of judgment and prejudice, coupled with a determination to take each child's agenda as the starting point, helps to create a good quality play environment; an environment that offers adaptability to the children, and so encourages the process of compound flexibility. Through their empathy, and their ability to interpret the children's play cues effectively, playworkers are able to create strong trusting relationships, which in turn help to enhance the children's self-esteem. If such approaches were applied universally, children might be expected to cope well with their immediate world, and also to develop naturally. This straightforward playwork approach works well across diverse settings including adventure playgrounds, after-school clubs, hospitals, and prisons. It is an approach that has even worked in Romania with some of the most play-deprived children in the world (Brown and Webb 2005). Consequently, within the play-deprived context of our contemporary society, incorporating a playwork approach across childhood settings seems essential.

Part 1
Debates, Dilemmas and Challenges: The Background to Children's Play

What is Play?

1

Chapter Outline

Introduction and key questions

Due to its positive impact on healthy child development, play has been identified as a basic human right for every child by the United Nations High Commission for Human Rights. Viewed through a broad lens, the play of children has been conceptualized across various domains including creativity, adaptation, exploration, experimentation, learning, communication, socialization, acculturation, and mastery (Piaget 1962; Schwartzman 1978; Vygotsky 1978). According to Glover (1999), play from a social constructivist perspective allows children to build and extend their knowledge and skills through interactions with the environment and other players. Sutton-Smith (1999) would agree and found that when children play, they re-create their worlds to make them less frightening and less mundane.

Common characteristics describe children's play as actively engaging, imaginative and creative, fluid and active, freely chosen, motivating, opportunistic and episodic, pleasurable, and most often more concerned with means than ends (Rubin, Fein, & Vandenberg 1983; Sturgess 2003). When applying these characteristics in play children enjoy what they are doing; use their imaginations when choosing how to play and what to play with; engage in pretense; and are more concerned with how they are playing than with the outcomes.

The subject of inclusion and exclusion of play in the lives of children is an important topic of inquiry in modern times. Many children today are being raised in an increasingly hurried and pressured lifestyle that limits the positive outcomes often associated with child-initiated play. This pressured lifestyle may be most recognizable throughout our society's educational systems that have shifted to endorse prescriptive curricula where play is often left out in the cold (Hirsh-Pasek et al. 2009). As the value of play becomes more marginalized in our accountability-driven and risk-adverse society, teachers and parents are left questioning play's value and worth. It seems that in the eyes of teachers and parents, play has become a luxury the contemporary child can ill afford.

This chapter attempts to answer these complex issues by examining:

- What is play?
- What are the personal and social benefits of play?
- What new socio-cultural developments are challenging long-held assumptions about children's play?
- What impact is this having on the lives of children?

What is play?

Archaeologists have documented the existence of play for thousands of years. This genealogy is depicted in the artifacts, paintings, and writings of primitive peoples across various cultures. In his work, *Theories of Play*, Brehony (2008) identifies prominent thinkers throughout history and their views and theories concerning play. These are summarized below. Although the summary is not exhaustive, it does provide a comprehensive account of how play has been defined across thousands of years. As you will see, many of the ideas and views expressed are in conflict with each other, making a common definition of play across the theories elusive.

Ancient Views

In ancient Greece, Plato recognized the significance of play in the lives of children even though the notion was somewhat taboo. In two prominent works, *The Laws* and *The Republic* Plato argues that play has a vital role in education; preparing children for life in the real world of adulthood. This adult centric view of play served as a means of controlling children. During this time it was commonly thought that free play would lead to negative outcomes for society. Holding such a view stands in opposition both to the notion of children learning and developing while they play, and also to the concept of play having aspects of both "being and becoming" (Sturrock 2007).

Enlightenment Views

Play viewed through the prism of religion has historically yielded negative connotations dating back to the Puritans and their strong ethic for work. In such societies it was common to hinder activities encouraging frivolity, which was generally thought to be the work of Satan. Somewhat ironically, it was a Puritan who initially advanced the idea that play should hold a prominent role in educating the young. In *Some Thoughts Concerning Education*, John Locke advocated the radical idea that children's education would be richer if learning was made to be a recreation. The empiricist theory of knowledge advanced by Locke made significant contributions to the notions that children learn through the senses and that childhood was a distinct and important period in human development.

The empiricist views of Locke inspired the enlightenment era philosopher Jean-Jacques Rousseau. In his classic text *Emile*, Rousseau advanced the radical theory that children progress through specific stages as they develop and that for education to be meaningful for children it should be in tune with those distinct stages. Rousseau found games and the social interactions between children engaged in those games to be fertile ground for learning. His idea that children should find learning pleasurable stood in stark contrast to the Puritan doctrine of schooling endorsed at this time.

Romantic Views

Play examined through the lens of the romantic period was strongly influenced by the views of Rousseau who believed in the concept of childhood innocence, and education following nature's lead. A strong proponent of this philosophy was Friedrich Froebel, founder of the kindergarten movement in Germany whose ideas, practices, and writings positioned play at the center of his educational theory, and suggested it was of the deepest significance. This view was a major departure from previous beliefs that thought play was trivial. Opportunities for children's play in the Froebelian kindergarten were controlled through his gifts and occupations.

Evolutionary Theories

The seminal work of English Naturalist Charles Darwin served as the spring-board for several evolutionary instrumentalist theories of play across species. The three prominent theories of the time were surplus energy, preparation for life, and race recapitulation. The initial theories offering scientific explanations of play, rather than previous observational and practical applications of its use, came into prominence after the publication of Darwin's *On the Origin of Species*.

The surplus energy theory of play advanced by Friedrich von Schiller and Herbert Spencer was an attempt to conceptualize the play of animals and argued that the highly developed nervous systems of species who are better equipped to meet with the necessities of life and survival expended surplus energy in the form of play. Play as preparation for later life was a second evolutionary theory of play based upon the work of Darwin advanced during the nineteenth century by Karl Groos. Groos argued that play contained an instinctual element that proved vital to the survival of any species, and that engaging in play helped to hone these survival skills. Play fighting among the young of many species is often cited as an example of this theory. The third prominent evolutionary theory of play during the late nineteenth century advanced by psycholo-gists James Baldwin and G. Stanley Hall was race recapitulation. This theory advances the idea that the development of each individual repeats the stages of development of human kind. And in contrast to play as preparation for life that stressed the honing of skills, in recapitulation theory play is not seen as an activity that builds future instinctual skills, but rather that it serves to free the organism of primitive instinctual skills passed down through heredity.

Scientific Theories

The theories of play advanced by John Dewey and Maria Montessori are considered scientific in nature due to their reliance on detailed observation and continuous experimentation. Dewey saw play as a subconscious activity that helped children develop cognitive and social competence. He further believed that play should be seperate from work as play helps the child transition into the world of work as an adult. Dewey held that as children became adults they relied less on play and instead found enjoyment in their chosen occupation. Play then prepares children to become working adults.

Where Dewey viewed play and work as binary opposites, the theory of education advanced by Maria Montessori blurred the lines between the two as articulated in her famous saying "play is the child's work." For Montessori children learned best by experiencing things as opposed to fantasizing about them, better know as sensory learning. In fact, Montessori held that fantasy play was the byproduct of a learning environment void of meaningful activities. Montessori also drew a distinction between the ideas of fantasy and imagination. During the late nineteenth century, fantasy was more associated with daydreaming, whereas imagination was employing facts to create something new. Therefore the Montessori classrooms are stocked with real objects for children to manipulate. Hence, a rich learning environment leads to a greater desire to learn.

Psychoanalytic Theories

In 1920 Sigmund Freud introduced his psychoanalytic theory of play in the important text *Beyond the Pleasure Principle*. Freud's theory views play as a mechanism for continually working out traumatic events experienced in the past in an effort to gain mastery of those events. Freud viewed this repetition as a child's way of reducing tension produced in daily life, or the pleasure principle. Eventually the pleasure principle of which play is a major part is replaced by the reality principle when the instinctual drives of children are replaced with the ability to reason.

Psychological Theories

The prominent psychological play theorists of the twentieth century include the Swiss psychologist Jean Piaget, the Russian psychologist Lev Vygotsky, and American psychologist Jerome Bruner. Their theories of play were unique in that they focused on cognitive functions of play.

For Piaget, play was defined as assimilation, or the child's attempts to match environmental stimuli to his or her own concepts. Piagetian theory argues that play itself does not result in the creation of new cognitive structures. Rather, Piaget believed that play was just for pleasure and while it provided children with opportunities to practice previous learnings, it did not necessarily result in the learning of new ideas. Through this lens, play is thought of as a process reflective of the beginning of symbolic development, but one that contributes little to it.

In contrast, Vygotskian theory holds that play actually facilitates cognitive development. Through play, children not only practice what they already know, they also learn new things. Vygotsky, who focused his definition of play on dramatic and make-believe play, saw play as the leading source of development in the preschool years. He believed that children developed higher mental functions through dramatic and make-believe play. Such playful activities allowed children to go beyond the level of learning they achieved previously.

In Bruner's theory, play was a means for acquiring information about and experience with the environment. Acquiring such information was vital in developing flexibility that allows for creativity. For Bruner, play provides the stage for children to experiment with combinations of behaviors that may otherwise never be explored. Social play experiences such as these serve as a communication system and the accompanying behaviors as transmitting messages, both of which aid in the development of social communication.

Contemporary Theories

In terms of prominent, contemporary play theorists, Brian Sutton-Smith (1997) finds an absolute definition of play to be elusive. As he once joked, "any earnest definition of play has to be haunted by the possibility that playful enjoinders will render it invalid" (1997, p. 213), and Sutton-Smith's own work has frequently presented such enjoinders. Sutton-Smith suggests that play can only be defined insofar as the rhetoric of a particular field or discipline allows. In his seminal work, *The Ambiguity of Play*, Sutton-Smith sets up a general theoretical framework for how people talk about play and games, that he called the seven rhetorics of play. In the book he sets out to explore the various discourses that emphasize the *irrationality* of play including children's play, adult play and animal play. Sutton-Smith observed that when most scholars talked about play, they fundamentally presupposed it to be either a form of progress, an exercise in power, a reliance on fate, a claim for identity, a form of frivolity, an issue of the imagination, or a manifestation of personal experience. His argument held that play was ambiguous, and the evidence for that ambiguity lay in these quite different scholarly ways of viewing play. After years of study, Sutton-Smith came to the conclusion that much of play was by itself intentionally ambiguous regardless of these seven general cultural frames.

Example of research:

Sutton-Smith (1997) identified seven rhetorics of play that he classified as either ancient or modern. The ancient rhetorics included fate, power, identity, and frivolity, with the modern forms being progress, the imaginary, and the self—as seen below.

1 The rhetoric of progress. Progress has proven to be a common element when studying the play of children. This rhetoric views play as a developmental arena, where children prepare for adulthood.

⇨

2 The rhetoric of fate. This rhetoric is older than the rest and dates back to mythologies where humans were controlled by destiny, gods, or luck.

3 The rhetoric of power. Power is the basis for competitions, and this stance holds that play is an expression of conflict. This rhetoric stands in opposition to modern theories of play focusing on leisure and progress.

4 The rhetoric of identity. Sutton-Smith's use of cultural identity here stresses social and cultural roles and structures. The focus is on communal identity rather than with the individual.

5 The rhetoric of the imaginary. The imaginary feeds creativity and flexibility and is sustained by current positive attitudes about creativity and innovation.

6 The rhetoric of the self. This rhetoric is often associated with solitary activities and associated with fun, relaxation, and escape. The central focus of this rhetoric is the player, and thus it appeals to modern influences of individuality and consumerism.

7 The rhetoric of frivolity. Frivolity applies to absurdity and the historical roles of tricksters and fools.

Reflections on the research

The Ambiguity of Play (1997) is the most comprehensive literature review concerning the various theories of play ever undertaken. Introducing the ambiguities of play to the reader is very useful in interpreting the scope and flexibility of both play as a concept, as well as Sutton-Smith's analysis. It explores the question of what the levels of play are, the kinds of play there are, and so on.

Activity 1

Play is reflective of the context in which it takes place (Bateson 1955). After visiting a variety of play environments, identify and reflect upon the way in which the environments affect the types of play you identify through the lens of the seven rhetorics.

Interview with Brian Sutton-Smith about his research

Brian Sutton-Smith, Emeritus Professor University of Pennsylvania

Michael Patte: **What were you trying to find out when you began working on the literature study that provides the grounding for *The Ambiguity of Play*?**

Brian Sutton-Smith: I was aware that none of the studies of children's play—and there were plenty—offered a credible definition of play. There were plenty of descriptions, but nothing that would do as a definition. So, I set out to collect every kind of play I could find to see whether I could identify commonalities within them. I found 308 different types of play, and I grouped them under seven headings, which I called the rhetorics of play.

Within these I found modern forms and ancient forms. Modern forms are the ones where people talk about psychological development, the imagination, and subjectivity of the agent—the self (that modern preoccupation with ontology). Then we get the ancient ones, which have been around much longer. The main one is all about contests, but also there are play forms that are about membership, and some that are about risk—gambling, and jumping off mountains, parachuting and so on. And finally there is nonsense and that's for the tricksters.

In my conclusion I placed a lot of emphasis on flexibility, and I suggested that play might be seen as the potentiation of adaptive variability; in other words, the mechanism by which the human species manages to cope with an ever-changing world.

Michael Patte: **Looking back, how do you think your own childhood experiences shaped your approach to children's play?**

Brian Sutton-Smith: I think they helped me to avoid the very common mistake of idealizing children's play. For example, we played a great game involving cow pots. Now a cow pot is a big round cow poop that dries on the surface but is still soft and sloppy underneath. These were our weapons. You put your hand on top, scooped it out on the dry part, and then threw it at each other's faces. Often it would break and get on your clothes and your mother would go nuts. Horse dung grenades were a pretty good weapon as well.

The famous anthropologist Robert Fagen described my view of play as earthy, physical, rough-edged, mischievous, subversive, competitive, occasionally cruel, not always fun, rarely lyrical and sometimes violent. I like that. Too many play theorists concentrate on the aspects of play that are acceptable to adults and for some reason they want to ignore the crude and cruel aspects of play. They are happy to talk about sweet little rhymes like *Oranges & Lemons*, but tend to shy away from the fact that children also recite rhymes like, *Listen my children and you shall hear of the midnight ride of diarrhea. Hasten Jason get the basin, oops plop get the mop.* Folklorists don't make that mistake. They study their subject, warts and all.

Michael Patte: **Tell us about the importance of folklore studies in shaping your thinking about play.**

Brian Sutton-Smith: The really exciting thing that came my way was the work of Peter and Iona Opie. I met Peter in a bar when I first went to England in the early 1950s. He and his wife had written books about the history of literature for children. Apparently there was literature for kids to read way back for about a thousand years. He and I got talking, and I had just finished my thesis, 900 pages of the games of New Zealand children, and he said "we don't have anything about play", so I talked him into doing play and they came out with the book *The Language and Lore of School Children*. What excited me later on was the way the contents in their book fitted the six or seven categories that I've been talking about—the rhetorics. The way they related the emotions to particular kinds of play behavior was a validation that hit me over the head with a big bang.

So, I joined the folklore people. Actually I co-created the Children's Folklore Society because I found that I could learn more about gangs talking to folklore people than to psychologists. Psychologists are trapped by their own need for an experiment. Good or bad as it may be, it doesn't take you to the world, whereas folklore is about traditions wherever they are.

Michael Patte: **How has your thinking evolved since publishing** *The Ambiguity of Play?*

Brian Sutton-Smith: I have worked up a pending book called *Play as Emotional Survival*. I will argue in that book that my rhetorics may be lined up alongside Damasio's primary and secondary emotions. I will also argue that if we want to think about play we have to think about it as more of a mythology, and that we need to identify the links between play and narrative, and play and humor.

When researchers study children's perceptions of play, they typically examine perceptions of work as well in order to offer a contrast. An important idea about children's perceptions of play and work revealed from research is that the perceptions of children and adults concerning play and work are often different. For example, Robson (1993) found from talking with children about their perceptions of play and work that they had learned through experience to associate play with their own self-initiated tasks, contrasting this with formal work involving teacher direction. Keating, Fabian, Jordan, Mavers, & Roberts (2000) supported this view by highlighting how children had a clear awareness of the difference between play and work, specifically with reference to varying learning opportunities inherent in them. In addition, two vital play elements identified by children in a study by King (1979) were the ability to choose and then to direct the activity. In a study of kindergarten and first/second graders' perceptions of play in a suburban primary school, Wing (1995) found that teachers tried to make work seem "play like," but children recognized this as disguised work. Both choice and direction were necessary components for an activity to be labeled as play for children in this study as well.

What are the personal and social benefits of play?

From ancient philosophy to current empirical research, play has been viewed as an enjoyable aspect of childhood that provides children with essential developmental benefits and opportunities for families to connect with their children. Research suggests that play is vital for cognitive, creative, emotional, physical, and social development, and that these developmental benefits last through adulthood.

Examples of research:

A study conducted by Ramstetter, Murray, & Garner (2010) from the *Journal of School Health* examined the value of recess as an integral component of the school day. Using Google Scholar, a review of the current recess literature was conducted to analyze definitions, position statements, and policy recommendations from both national and international associations and organizations. Results from the study identified crucial factors for recess to reach its full potential at school. These included that recess was well supervised by trained play leaders and that the play environment was safe and well maintained. When these conditions were met, opportunities for daily recess proved beneficial for children's cognitive, social, emotional, and physical development. The study further found recess to serve as a necessary break from the daily academic rigors of the school day. The authors found recess and the unstructured free play taking place there to provide a unique contribution to the creative, social, and emotional development of children—a time that should not be withheld for academic or punitive reasons.

Reflections on the research

Ironically, a main reason often stated for eliminating child-initiated free play from the lives of children—improved academic achievement—may actually be counterproductive to achieve the goal. Recent evidence suggests that unstructured play promotes

---

and enhances physical health, as well as social, emotional, and cognitive development (Barros, Silver, & Stein 2009; Kahan 2008; Robert Wood Johnston Foundation 2007). Free play is fundamental to the healthy development of the whole child (American Academy of Pediatrics 2006). Throughout the school day, recess provides daily opportunities to enhance these vital developmental needs. The evidence is clear in stating that the benefits of providing children with time for daily child-initiated, unstructured play far outweighs the costs (National Association for Sport and Physical Education 2004).

Activity 2

The examples of research draw on findings that suggest children, after play, "are focused in class and better able to attend to academic tasks" and that "unstructured play provides opportunities for children to develop social skills that are not acquired in more formal classroom environments." From your own experiences of play, your memories of play, or observations of children at play: (1) Why do you think play might offer these benefits? (2) What qualities of "unstructured play" might be important to these areas of benefit and opportunity for children?

Cognitive benefits

In terms of academic achievement and cognitive development, play helps children adjust to the school environment, enhance school readiness, learning behaviors, and problem-solving skills (Milteer & Ginsburg 2012).

Examples of research:

A 2004 study by Fantuzzo, Sekino, & Cohen examined relationships between two samples of urban Head Start children's peer play competence and other relevant competencies. Elements of peer play were analyzed along with emotional regulation, autonomy, and language. Children displaying high levels of peer play interaction demonstrated greater emotional regulation, initiation, self-determination, and receptive vocabulary skills. Evidence of positive engagement in play early in the year were associated with lower levels of aggressive, shy, and withdrawn adjustment problems at the end of the year. Children who experienced positive interactions with peers early in the year realized greater cognitive outcomes.

Reflections on the research

When playing, children gain knowledge, rehearse new skills, and enhance readiness skills and learning behaviors that ultimately provide the foundation to develop academic success (McWayne et al. 2004). Research by Ginsburg et al. (2005) suggests that young children who engaged daily in spontaneous play are building the foundation for early mathematical reasoning through exploring concepts like shape, space, pattern, and numbers found in everyday surroundings. Further, Schulz & Bonawitz (2007) argue that children use play to test and develop hypotheses and to grapple with problems they encounter in their world. For example, when children are introduced to a new toy, the first thing they do, without adult intervention, is to figure out how the toy works through exploration. In addition, through symbolic play, children engage in imaginative, role-taking scenarios when playing with objects (Tamis-LeMonda et al. 2002). That type of play encourages a broad range of activities ranging from employing common objects and scenarios to fantasy-driven roles and contexts. The cognitive effects of symbolic play are profound and include enhanced abstract thought (Saltz, Dixon & Johnson 1977), symbolic representation (DeLoache 2002), perspective taking (Youngblade & Dunn 1995), creativity (Russ, Robins, & Christiano 1999), memory (Newman 1990), intelligence (Johnson, Ershler, & Lawton 1982), language (Pellegrini & Galda 1993), and literacy (Nicolopoulou, McDowell & Brockmeye 2006).

Activity 3

Play is often trivialized as being frivolous, unproductive, and a general waste of time. Using the research cited above, compose an "elevator speech" to convince a naysayer about the positive impact of play on the cognitive development of children. (An elevator speech is a short summary used to quickly define a position and its value.)

Creative benefits

Children today engage in many activities but many of them, like organized sports and music lessons, are cutting into time for free play. But such experiences have a priori rules that are determined in advance. Free play, on the other hand, does not have a priori rules, so it offers opportunities for children to use and develop their creativity. This creative aspect is crucial because it provides challenge to the developing brain more than following predetermined rules does. In free play, children experiment with new activities and roles.

Examples of research:

A classic study by Dansky & Silverman (1973) conducted with ninety preschool children examined the impact of play on creative thinking. Researchers divided the participants into three groups. The first group was instructed to play freely with four common objects (paper towels, a screwdriver, a wooden board, a pile of paper clips). The second group was instructed to imitate a researcher using the objects in certain ways. The third group was instructed to sit at a table and draw a picture of their choice without ever viewing the objects. All three of the activities were ten minutes long. Immediately following each of the activities the researchers asked the participants to invent ways that one of the four objects could be used. The children who had freely played with the objects identified three times as many non-standard uses for the objects compared with participants in either of the other two groups, suggesting that free play is associated with creativity.

Reflections on the research

Largely in the United States and United Kingdom, traditional notions of childhood with plenty of space and time for child-initiated discovery, unstructured play, art, and music have disappeared and been replaced by adult-directed structured activities both in the classroom and in the living room (Miller & Almon 2009). Dana Gioia, former chairman for the National Endowment of the Arts, believes that "adult life begins in a child's imagination" and that in modern-day society "we've relinquished that imagination to the marketplace." Miller & Almon (2009) agree:

> The withering of imagination in childhood is a looming catastrophe with consequences as profound as global climate change, but much less widely recognized. The very attributes we most want to nurture in our children— creativity, initiative, collaboration, problem-solving, courage—are best developed through imaginative play (p.72).

Activity 4

Consider the summary and findings of the Dansky & Silverman research:

How do you think the children might have seen/understood what they were being asked to do?
What different understandings of the findings might there be? For example, do you think the way children understood the first part of the research activity (why they were being asked to draw, watch an adult play in a certain way, or play with objects) might affect their response to the second part of the research?
What do you think the research might tell us about adult attitudes towards research and children?
How do you see the idea of creativity being interpreted within this research—what is being seen as creative or not creative?

Emotional benefits

Play allows children to create and explore a world they can control, overcoming their fears while carrying out adult roles, often in collaboration with peers or adult caregivers (Hurwitz 2003). As children begin mastering their world, play helps them to acquire new skills that provide a wellspring of confidence and resiliency needed to face future challenges (Marano 2008). Children's contact with the outdoors and exploring the natural environment contributes to their emotional and psychological well-being through letting off steam, shouting and running, quiet reflection, confiding in others, and being with family members and pets (Thomas & Thompson 2004).

Example of research:

The *Journal of Child Psychology and Psychiatry* published a study in 1984 that assessed the anxiety levels of seventy-four three- and four-year-old children on their first day of preschool. Their levels of stress were measured by three distinct behaviors—whether they pleaded, whined and begged their parents to stay—and how much their palms were sweating. Based on observations, the researchers labeled each child as either anxious or not anxious. They then randomly split the seventy-four children into four groups. Half of the children were placed in rooms full of toys, where they played either alone or with peers for fifteen minutes; the other half were instructed to sit at a small table either alone or with peers and listen to a fifteen-minute story told by a teacher.

Afterward, the children's levels of anxiety were assessed again. The stress levels of the anxious children who played had dropped by more than twice as much as compared with the anxious children who had listened to the story. (The children who were not anxious to begin with remained about the same.) Interestingly, those who played alone calmed down more than the ones who played with peers. The researchers speculate that through imaginative play, which is most easily initiated alone, children build fantasies that help them cope with difficult situations.

Reflections on the research

When children play together they realize a variety of socio-emotional benefits. For example, social play provides children with opportunities to subordinate personal desires to social rules, willingly cooperate with others, and to exhibit socially acceptable behavior (Berk et al. 2006). Further, fantasy play has been shown to be vital for developing children's social competence, including the ability to self-soothe and cope emotionally with stressful situations (Connolly & Doyle 1984). Animal research also highlights the therapeutic benefits of play for relieving stress. In neuroscience, the concept is known as social buffering. Evolutionary biologist Marc Bekoff (2009) compares play to a kaleidoscope in that it is somewhat random and creative. He further asserts that play fosters creativity and flexibility that will be of enormous benefit when children encounter unexpected situations or strange environments.

Activity 5

If you work with children, create an arrangement whereby you can observe children playing over the course of a week. Identify common themes across the various types of play observed. Reflect upon the therapeutic benefits that certain play themes offer to the children. Are these therapeutic benefits observable across all types of play?

Physical benefits

Play builds active healthy bodies. Research by the Center for Disease Control and Prevention (2005) reveals that the prevalence of childhood obesity is on the rise and increasingly sedentary lifestyles are partially to blame. According to the US Department of Health and Human Services (2008), daily physical activity in the form of play helps control weight, builds lean muscle, reduces fat, and contributes to a healthy functioning cardiovascular system, hormonal regulatory system and immune system; promotes strong bone, muscle and joint development; and decreases the risk of obesity (American Academy of Pediatrics 2006). Further, with the heightened control of the body developed through play, children often improve their skills and gain self-confidence to play games with friends (Wortham 2006).

Example of research:

A 2010 study in the *International Journal of Behavioral Nutrition and Physical Activity* investigated the association between a range of recess variables such as children's sedentary, moderate, and vigorous physical activity. One hundred and twenty-eight children between the ages of nine and ten from eight elementary schools had their physical activity levels measured during recess using the System for Observing Children's Activity and Relationships during Play (SOCARP). Multilevel prediction models highlighted variables significantly related to children's activity levels during recess.

In addition, children lacking equipment during recess engaged in more sedentary activity and less moderate activity than children with access to playground equipment. Further, as children were provided with more space to play sedentary activity decreased and vigorous activity increased. The authors argue that several factors influence children's choice of involvement in sedentary, moderate, and vigorous physical activity levels during recess including access to playground equipment and plenty of physical space to play.

Reflections on the research

Physical movement is correlated with the growth and development of the mind as well as the body. In order to function properly the brain needs movement (Tamis-LeMonda et al. 2004). Outdoor environments provide the optimum amount of space for the types of physical activities children need daily. Outdoor play encourages the types of physical activity associated with improving children's health. According to Sutterby and Frost (2002), outdoor recess periods provide the time and space children need to participate in physically active play.

Activity 6

If you work with children, create an arrangement whereby you can observe children playing in a variety of settings and analyze variables that impact their activity levels (sedentary, moderate, vigorous) during play. How do your findings compare with those from the study highlighted above?

Traditional approaches have involved adults designing play spaces for children without engaging with children themselves. What do you think this research reveals about such traditions?

Social benefits

Play appears to assist in the development of strong social skills. Children do not become socially competent by having adults telling them how to behave. Rather, they learn those skills through meaningful interactions with their peers where they learn what is acceptable and what is not. Children quickly learn that to keep a game going they need to accommodate the other players' desires. Due to the strong intrinsic motivation associated with play, children are apt to stick it out even in the face of frustration that helps to develop persistence and negotiating skills. Playing with peers enhances arguably the most important social skill, communication. In fact, research suggests that children's language use is more sophisticated when playing with other children compared with adults (Elias & Arnold 2006).

What new socio-cultural developments are challenging long-held assumptions about children's play?

The sights and sounds of children playing outdoors are a hallmark of any thriving, robust community. However, due to a variety of current, societal factors devaluing play, many opportunities for children's play have been lost in Western societies. These factors that serve as barriers to play include fear, access to quality play spaces, increased amounts of screen time, and a reduction in school-based playtime.

Culture of Fear

Present day scholars (Marano 2008; Elkind 2007; Patte 2010b) document fragility and weaknesses in children who are prevented from experiencing any risky activity by overbearing parents. These parents discourage children from exploring the outside world in their neighborhood for fear of being abducted; forbid children to engage in rough-and-tumble play that requires physical contact with other players for fear they might be injured; and intervene on their behalf in the most frivolous of disputes. In this sheltered world children are kept from experiencing sensations that were common only forty years ago. Preventing children from experiencing these joyful excursions can impair their resilience.

Research documents the disappearance of play in the streets and in children playing outside (Gill 2007b; Kinoshita 2008; Van Gils et al. 2009). Singer et al. (2009) surveyed mothers from sixteen countries in Africa, Asia, Europe, North America and South America, and found a perceived reduction in spontaneous opportunities for play during the past twenty years. Across all countries mothers cited fear of children playing out, of getting dirty, of contacting germs, of crime, and of traffic. Fear of violence, street crime, discrimination, and harassment is a global problem (Bartlett 2002; Chawla 2002b).

How can this overwhelming fear that cripples parents be managed and allow children to reconnect with outdoor play spaces? One possible remedy would be for outdoor play spaces to be manned by trained professional staff. Training programs in playwork are prominent throughout north European countries, and are beginning to gain steam in Japan. UK universities offer degree programs in playwork. For example Leeds Metropolitan University in the UK has been offering higher education qualifications since 1989. Once certified, these playworkers facilitate play and oversee play spaces across a variety of play settings ranging from adventure playgrounds to after-school clubs. During the early part of the twentieth century many universities across America offered a similar type of training program for play leaders called the Normal Course on Play, which was designed to train play leaders in program planning, the nature and function of play, play leadership, play facilities, organization and administration, and the history of the community recreation movement (Frost 2010). Although this course has been abandoned for decades, programs for training playworkers in America are beginning to sprout up at universities, children's museums, and park and recreation centers. This grassroots movement endorses the basic right of children to engage in outdoor play.

Activity 7

Interview someone over the age of 45 about their play experiences as a child and compare those experiences with someone under the age of 25. What influence does the culture of fear barrier have on the experiences of both people? What strategies would you employ to overcome the present-day culture of fear?

Access to play spaces

Example of research:

Gaining access to quality play spaces is a second barrier impacting opportunities for play in America. Grow et al. (2008), in research conducted for the Department of Pediatrics at the University of Washington, studied three major cities in the US. They examined factors related to two sources of physical activity for youth: active use of recreation sites and active transport to recreation sites. Eighty-seven parents of children and one hundred twenty-four matched pairs of parents and adolescents in three US cities reported on youths' active use of, proximity to, and walking/biking to twelve recreation sites and on neighborhood walkability and safety. Multivariate regression models evaluated factors associated with youths' frequent site use and active transport to sites.

Results suggest that neighborhoods encouraging physical activity for children had more playgrounds and neighborhood characteristics that provided ease of access to the playgrounds including higher street connectivity, lower traffic, less crime, and better aesthetics. Neighborhoods with at least five playgrounds boasted street connectivity that was 13.5 per cent higher, traffic was 7 per cent lower, crime was 9.6 per cent lower, and the aesthetics were 15 per cent better compared to neighborhoods with fewer than five playgrounds (Grow et al. 2008).

There appear to be socioeconomic and race/ethnic disparities when attempting to access a variety of physical activity facilities. A national study suggests that lower median income areas with higher percentages of minorities were less likely to have access to gyms, health clubs, and YMCAs. With limited access to such fee-based facilities, gaining access to free facilities like parks and playgrounds becomes increasingly important for minority populations (Gordon-Larsen et al. 2006). In addition to the disparities in access, research suggests there are also inequities related to the safety of playgrounds. A study by Cradock et al. (2005) found that playgrounds in predominantly Black impoverished neighborhoods were less safe compared to those in other neighborhoods.

Activity 8

Poll a segment of parents about access to outdoor play spaces in your local community. How do your results compare with the national statistics from the United States found above? What factors might be common, what might be different, in relation to various communities and children's access to play spaces? Think about issues raised in this section and how you understand commonalities and differences.

Increasing amounts of screen time

In recent years it seems that time spent in front of screens (televisions, computers, cell phones, etc.) has all but replaced opportunities for children to engage in active, social, and creative play (Ravichandran & France de Bravo 2010). Today play often takes place at home in isolation. The sedentary pursuits of children at home engaged with electronic media contribute greatly to inactivity and recent studies suggest that children between 10–16 years of age engage in vigorous activity for thirteen minutes each day and spend over ten of their waking hours virtually motionless. Fed by concerns about sexual predators and other hazards, parents are often relieved to have children at home engaged in various electronic media. However, this lack of contact time with other social beings may rob children of opportunities to learn social skills through face-to-face play in more social settings (Frost 2010).

The pros and cons of technology play are well studied. Singer and Singer (2005) examined the effects of electronic media on children's cognitive and moral development and documented that the drastic effects of violence in the media are now a reality. However, they suggest that with proper supervision from trusted adults, electronic media can exert a positive influence on the development of the whole child. While the findings concerning adult monitored play and learning are positive, they should not discount the volume of findings that confirm the severe consequences of affording children complete freedom in accessing electronic media (Frost 2010).

Decreasing amounts of school-based play time

The idea of offering a recess period as part of the school day is a time-honored tradition. These breaks during the school day provide a brief respite from the academic rigors and allow time for physical and social rejuvenation. However, today that tradition has been called into question. The reason most often cited for the reduction or elimination of the recess period is that it is a waste of valuable time that could be more wisely used for instruction. This reallocation of time argument has gained considerable traction in the US and the UK and has put the playtime/recess period at risk.

In America, a nationally representative survey of school districts conducted by the Center on Education Policy (2007) reported that roughly 20 per cent of districts shortened the recess period by an average of fifty minutes per week to provide additional English and math instructional time (McMurrer 2007). Research suggests that the recess period in the US is offered sporadically and that as children progress from primary school to elementary school, time for recess wanes (Lee et al. 2007). In addition to reducing recess time for additional instruction, it is also often withheld from students as punishment for not complying with school rules (Lee et al. 2006). These findings are troublesome due to the multifaceted beneficial outcomes associated with offering a daily recess period including academic, cognitive, emotional, physical, and social benefits. These benefits are underscored by the recommendations for daily, unstructured recess periods for all children by the Centers for Disease Control and Prevention (CDC), National Association for Sports and Physical Education, and National Association of Early Childhood Specialists in State Departments of Education (4–6).

Activity 9

Interview a veteran teacher about the status of recess in the present day classroom. Determine if recess has been an important element of the school day during the past 25–30 years. Have attitudes towards recess changed during that time? If so, what societal factors have influenced the change?

What impact is this having on the lives of children?

There is mounting research across multiple disciplines that links negative responses to the play agenda to negative impact on children:

- *Lacking social competence*—Depriving children of opportunities for free outdoor play restricts their ability to gather and socialize spontaneously with peers. Lacking this ability can impede the development of social-emotional learning, social interactions, communication skills, and self-control (National Association of Early Childhood Specialists in State Departments of Education 2002).

- *Incidence of Attention Deficit Hyperactive Disorder (ADHD)*—Due in part to an increasing emphasis on academic achievement in schools and compacting of curriculum into early childhood classrooms causing children to sit idly by for extended periods of time, Marano (2008) reports skyrocketing numbers of children now requiring medication to get through childhood. For example, in the USA over twenty-one million prescriptions are written each year for stimulant drugs to enhance attention, mostly in children ages 6–14, a 400 per cent increase over a decade.

- *Child fragility*—According to Marano (2008), when parents deflect the discomfort, the disappointment, and the opportunities for play out of the lives of their children, especially while increasing the pressure for success, they can cause great harm. In such an environment children lack the necessary challenges to sharpen their instincts and are unequipped to create their own strategies for dealing with the uncertainties of life.

- *Health concerns*—Children throughout the world are confronting the epidemic of childhood obesity and during the last four decades in the US, the obesity rate for children ages 6–11 has more than quadrupled. For adolescents (12–19 years of age) the number has more than tripled (Ogden et al. 2010). Currently, more than twenty-three million young people in America are considered overweight or obese.

- *Incidence of anxiety and depression*—When children are deprived of the opportunity to play, they miss out on nature's best antidote for depression. Panksepp (2002) argues that play serves as the deepest wellspring of joy in the human experience which insulates us from anxiety and depression.

- *Decrease in creativity and imagination*—If children are overly restricted in the ability to play freely outdoors, they tend to become risk-adverse and overly cautious. Such behaviors can have a negative impact on their ability to solve problems, also known as divergent thinking. Recent studies have tracked a steady decline in childhood creativity and although there is probably no single cause, researchers cite lack of play as a significant mitigating factor (Marano 2008).

- *Inflexibility*—Research by Bekoff & Pierce (2009) identified a *"Flexibility Hypothesis"* which holds that animals are able to switch and improvise all behaviors more effectively through play. Further, they advocate the importance of play in developing creative and flexible children who are able to cope with unexpected situations and new environments.

- *Aversion to risk*—Marano (2008) accurately portrays an American landscape where many children are overprotected and overmanaged by their parents and kept from dealing with meaningful challenges with which to hone their instincts. In such an environment children are unable to adapt to a fluid environment making them risk-averse and psychologically fragile.

In Chapter 6 we make the argument that the field of playwork popular in the UK, Germany and some Scandinavian countries endorses a core set of principles that seem well suited to address many societal factors devaluing play in the lives of children throughout the world and provides an excellent medium to help rethink children's play.

Summary

This chapter has:

- offered a genealogy of play highlighting prominent cultures and scholars and their contributions in helping provide an answer to the question, what is play?
- examined the cognitive, creative, emotional, physical, and social benefits of play.
- explored current societal factors devaluing children's play and their impact on child development.
- touched upon the argument that the field of playwork and its guiding principles seemed well suited to address the societal factors devaluing children's play and provide the means to help rethink children's play.

Further reading

Brown, F. (ed.) (2003) *Playwork: Theory and Practice*. Buckingham: Open University Press. This book presents a range of theoretical and practical perspectives of playwork, with examples of playwork in practice, including adventure playgrounds, establishing play in a local authority, and a therapeutic playwork project with abandoned children in Romania.

Elkind, D. (2007) *The power of play: How spontaneous, imaginative activities lead to happier, healthier children*. Massachusetts: Da Capo Press. In defense of unstructured downtime, this book offers ways to restore play's vital role in the lives of children at home, at school, and in the larger community. It will help the reader to resist the proliferation of educational products and extracurricular activities aimed at monopolizing our children's childhoods.

Sutton-Smith, B. (1997) *The ambiguity of play*. Cambridge: Harvard University Press. An examination of play which suggests that play theories are rooted in seven distinct rhetorics—the ancient discourses of fate, power, communal identity, frivolity, and the modern discourses of progress, the imaginary and the self. The author leads us towards a new definition of play as the potentiation of adaptive variability.

Part 2
Contemporary Issues

Play and Schools

2

Chapter Outline

Introduction and key questions

Almost a century ago the famous educationalist Rudolf Steiner described how the souls of children seek to develop and unfold in accordance with their own nature. During this time there was an unparalleled interest in children's play. The play movement in the United States advanced the promotion of spontaneous play and the development of playgrounds throughout schoolyards. For example, a report of the 1940 White House Conference on Children and Youth (US Superintendent of Documents 1940, p.191) held, "All persons require types of experiences through which the elemental desire for friendship, recognition, adventure, creative expression, and group acceptance may be realized… Favorable conditions of play… contribute much toward meeting these basic emotional needs." The report further stated that play also enhances the growth and development of the child while at the same time promoting motor, manual, and artistic skills—all positions corroborated by research conducted throughout the latter half of the twentieth century.

Contrast this beautiful notion with the intensity of the educational culture pervasive in many Western schools today that now contributes to the suppression of curiosity, imagination, and fantasy. The mainstream education system seems to have lost sight of the developmental needs of children and instead is now advancing an adult-centered approach characterized by didactic, standardized curricula. Elkind (2008) points out that growing numbers of schools are eliminating creative and playful teaching practices and recess in favor of more time for academic learning. Miller & Almon (2009) echo these sentiments and state that children in early childhood education spend far more classroom time on literacy and math skills than they do learning through play and exploration. Further, they find that such practices are not supported by research and actually violate long-established child development and sound teaching principles.

This chapter seeks to tease out these two opposing views of the role of play in school through answering the following questions:

- How has the inclusion of play in school evolved over time?
- Is it possible to implement a playful pedagogy in a standards-driven society?
- How can we make the case for child-initiated unstructured play during the school day?

Activity 1

Play Memory:
Illustrate a detailed picture of a play memory from your childhood. Reflect upon how certain elements have changed over time. For instance, what elements of your play memory might be common/uncommon for young children today?

How has the inclusion of play in school evolved over time?

In his seminal text, *A History of Children's Play and Play Environments* (2010) Frost identifies two important movements emerging around the turn of the twentieth century in western society that provided an impetus for children to play: the physical fitness movement that emphasized physical development and recreation, and a heightened understanding of child development based on the work of prominent philosophers from the Renaissance era. The ideas endorsed in Froebel's kindergarten placed play as a central component of the child development movement and although play was not the sole focus on the movement, resulting research in the field was fundamental in positioning play as a vital component in the healthy development of children.

Play in Kindergarten

The first kindergartens (meaning "children's garden") were child-centered in their approach emanating from the natural curiosity of children. The classroom environment facilitated by the teacher stimulated the senses and guided the children toward self-direction and self-control (Frost 2010). The pedagogical approach employed prescribed materials known as the gifts (balls, blocks, cubes, etc.) and occupations (clay, wood carving, painting, weaving, etc.) and children's active involvement with them. All of the materials used in Froebel's kindergarten encouraged discovery and inventiveness.

At the birth of the twentieth century studies examining the theory and meaning of play, the relation between play and work, and the value of play in education were undertaken (Frost 2010). In 1907, George Ellsworth Johnson developed a play-based curriculum that provided a roadmap of the foundational play practices for western nursery schools, kindergartens, and primary schools of the early 1900s. Johnson held that both play and work could serve as complimentary elements in the education of young children and his curriculum provided developmentally appropriate activities to arouse their interests.

If we juxtapose the child-centered tenants of the Froebelian kindergartens described above with the teacher-directed ones found in many present-day programs, one can see how drastically things have changed in the past 175 years. In their recent report, *Crisis in the kindergarten: Why children need to play at school*, Miller and Almon (2009) document an alarming trend in kindergarten classrooms across America. The report sheds light on the disappearance of play in early education and kindergarten classrooms at an alarming rate. Today children spend far more time engaged with highly scripted, teacher directed curricula focusing on literacy and numeracy than they do through exploration and play. To highlight, children enrolled in all day kindergartens spend four to six times as much time engaged in formal instruction and in preparing for tests as they do engaged in free play or choice time (Miller & Almon 2009).

Many prominent early childhood programs throughout the world still recognize the importance of play as a vital component of the kindergarten curriculum. But according to Frost (2010) personal ideology and political motivations of the late twentieth and early twenty-first centuries threaten long established principles of child development and good teaching.

Example of research:

In their recent report *Crisis in the kindergarten: Why children need to play in school* Miller & Almon (2009) document the radical transformation of kindergarten in America over the past twenty years. They report that children now spend far more time being taught and tested on literacy and numeracy skills than they do learning exploration and play. Today many kindergartens endorse prescriptive curricula and teacher-directed pedagogical approaches which are not grounded on solid research and which stand in opposition to tenets of child development and sound teaching practices. Such approaches seem to be compromising children's long-term health and their opportunities for success in school. Miller & Almon (2009) implore policymakers, educators, health professionals, researchers, and parents to:

- Restore child-initiated play and experimental learning with the active support of teachers to their rightful place at the heart of kindergarten education.
- Reassess kindergarten standards to ensure that they promote developmentally appropriate practices, and eliminate those that do not.
- End the inappropriate use in kindergarten of standardized tests, which are prone to serious error especially when given to children under eight.
- Expand the early childhood research agenda to examine the long-term impact of current preschool and kindergarten practices on the development of children from diverse backgrounds.
- Give teachers of young children first-rate preparation that emphasizes the full development of the child and the importance of play, nurtures children's innate love of learning, and supports teachers' own capacities for creative autonomy and integrity.
- Use the crisis of play's disappearance from kindergarten to rally organizations and individuals to create a national movement for play in schools and communities.

Reflections on the research

The research offered in the Miller & Almon (2009) report suggests that current practices in many American kindergartens may cause high levels of frustration, stress, and anger among the children, leading to significant behavior problems. In addition to increasing academic pressure in the lives of children through endorsing developmentally inappropriate standards, the modern kindergarten philosophy has also robbed children of their most valuable tool for dealing with stress—play that is freely chosen, child-directed, and intrinsically motivated. Have current national legislative efforts in the United States in the form of No Child Left Behind and in the

United Kingdom in the form of Every Child Matters aimed at guaranteeing students' academic success at school discounted more developmentally appropriate practices? Research suggests that developmentally appropriate classrooms are not solely comprised of child-initiated activities (Bredekamp & Rosegrant 1995). These authors suggest that teachers should employ a variety of approaches that include aspects of direct, mediated, and non-direct instruction. Dewey (1916) offered a similar continuum including fooling-play-work-drudgery. Both of these models suggest that work and play can be successfully melded into a curriculum of appropriate practice for children.

Activity 2

What societal forces are impacting the endorsement of "prescriptive curricula and teacher directed pedagogical approaches" in kindergartens as described above? What arguments might be made in favor of such a direction for play within kindergartens? What kinds of influences, pressures, and needs might they be responding to? Further, what arguments might be made to counter "prescriptive curricula and teacher-directed pedagogical approaches" and what reasons might be given for an alternative approach such as "child-initiated play and experimental learning with the active support of teachers"?

Play Schools

Building on the momentum established by Johnson's play-based curriculum mentioned above, an innovative approach to educating children called the Demonstration Play School appeared in the early part of the twentieth century at the University of California. According to Frost (2010), the school's ambitious mission sought to combine two historically competing influences, the spontaneous play of children and the societal demand for education. Through this lens children were viewed as spontaneous, active, and driven by their internal needs. The three goals directing the Play School's mission identified by Frost (2010) include: (1) to organize activities for a complete play life; (2) to provide leadership so that the capacity for work may be established; and (3) to connect play with materials and activities for success in society. Common curricular activities implemented to stimulate the child's play life included environmental and nature activities, as well as time for indoor and outdoor play. Proponents of the Play School movement believed that children learned through living and participating in natural, everyday experiences and as children continued to grow and develop, these experiences were augmented with work actualized through academics (Frost 2010).

Although traces of the Play School philosophy are still being implemented in some early childhood programs endorsing certain pedagogical philosophies like Waldorf and Reggio Emilia, it never developed substantial traction in the American public school system. One possible reason offered by Frost (2010) revolves around stark differences in professional training of early childhood professionals (strong child development training) and elementary school teachers (training grounded in curriculum and instruction). This lack of traction for incorporating play in schools can be witnessed firsthand today as kindergarten children spend far more time being taught and tested on literacy and numeracy skills than they do learning through play and exploration, exercising their bodies, and using their imaginations (Miller & Almon 2009).

Pellegrini (2005) expresses a sense of amazement about the scant writings of the historical origins of recess in American schools. Some suggest that the limited scope offered to games, play, and recess in American research annals is partly attributable to our Puritan/Calvinist past. From this stance, the work ethic aligned with Calvinism has infiltrated the American culture and therefore many activities associated with leisure are marginalized. Due to this cultural norm, play is often marginalized in schools in many industrial societies. To see this phenomenon in action one has to look no farther than the playground during recess. Here the activities are truly play-like as children are relatively free to interact with friends and materials independently of adult intervention. It is the child-initiated, freely chosen nature of these playground activities that many adults view as impediments to a proper education.

Scholars conducting research on play in schools are often at odds and typically represent two distinct camps. The first sees play as a liberating force in school while the other views play as a means of controlling children at school (Pellegrini 2005).

School play as a liberating force

Play scholars like Sutton-Smith (1997) believe certain forms of play in schools can act as a liberating and creative process allowing children to transform common everyday situations in unexpected ways. Such a process provides a forum for children to think in more creative ways. However, for this process to take place, schools must provide children with ample time and space to act out their playful desires. Unfortunately, many present day schools are unwilling to dedicate time for such pursuits.

The field of folklore is rich with examples that suggest children's play at school during recess is an ideal setting for innovative thought (Blatchford 1998; Opie & Opie 1959). While examining the history of children's games, these folklore scholars found that children often bring to school the games learned in the private and secret spaces outside of school including local parks and neighborhoods. Combining these new variations of games with those present at school makes the school playground a fertile breeding ground for new forms of play (Pellegrini 2005).

The seminal work of prominent twentieth century play scholar and folklorist Brian Sutton-Smith further advances the idea that children's play and recess generate creativity. His colorful recollections of childhood in New Zealand complete with depictions of bawdy children engaged in various forms of frivolity are reminiscent of those depicted in Breughel's painting, *Children's Games* (Pellegrini 2005). Sutton-Smith depicts in rich detail how the New Zealand countryside melded with the school yard to create a space where children had their own culture and rules very different from those found in the classroom.

Example of research:

Many children today lead lives every bit as structured as those of adults. And although participating in games with rules provides a fun source of learning, they are also limiting due to their a priori rules. Child-initiated free play, which does not impose such a priori rules, affords children more creative responses. This creative aspect of play is vital as it challenges the developing brain to a greater extent than does following predetermined rules. In free play, children exercise their imagination, experiment with new activities, and develop new roles.

In a recent study Hoffman & Russ (2011) examined the relationship among pretend play, creativity, emotional regulation, and executive functioning in children. The processes of pretend play were assessed using the Affect in Play Scale (APS) which identifies the cognitive and affective processes of children. Sixty-one female students between the ages of five and ten were assessed using the APS to measure their pretend play ability, a divergent thinking task (the Alternative Uses Test), a storytelling task to assess creativity, an executive functioning measure (the Wisconsin Card Sorting Task), and parental report on the Emotional Regulation Checklist (ERC). Through the use of correlational analyses, pretend play significantly related to creativity as measured by storytelling and divergent thinking, and related to emotion regulation. Further, affect expression in play was significantly related to affect expression in storytelling which suggested cross-situational stability.

Divergent thinking was also significantly related to creativity in storytelling. The magnitudes of the correlations were in general of medium effect size. No significant relationships were identified with executive functioning. The study results suggest that play, creativity, and emotional regulation are linked.

Reflections on the research

The research study by Hoffman & Russ (2011) speaks to the positive aspects of pretend play in the development of creativity and emotional regulation. However, other recent studies have tracked a steady decline in childhood creativity and although there is no single cause, lack of play is cited as a mitigating factor (Marano 2008).

There is a common characteristic to play in all its protean forms—variety itself. In play, the sequence of actions is often fluid and scattered. Evolutionary biologist Marc Bekoff describes play as a behavioral kaleidoscope. In fact, it is this kaleidoscopic quality that helped researchers to find play as the most effective way for animals to gain a more diverse and responsive repertoire of behaviors—something Bekoff & Pierce (2009) termed a *"Flexibility Hypothesis"* which holds that animals are able to switch and improvise all behaviors more effectively through play.

If children are deprived of opportunities to engage in the types of play associated with the development of creativity, what implications might that hold for their physical, social, emotional, and creative well-being?

School play as a controlling force

The second view of play at school in many western societies focuses on controlling children's play (Pellegrini 2005). This happens when school personnel use children's play to actualize some ideal forms of behavior. Two ways this control is actualized on a daily basis in present-day schools is through restrictive playground rules governing children's behavior, and the practice of withholding recess due to poor behavior and poor academic achievement.

Cavallo (1981) documenting the history of the playground movement in America highlights how the birth of the playground movement coincided with the influx of immigration in the early 20th century. At this time a child saving movement was afoot led by prominent citizens in many American cities, with the goal of socializing immigrant children to become productive citizens. At the end of the nineteenth century, this control was exerted on playgrounds by play supervisors and social workers who taught children how to play and attempted to control their developing social skills (Pellegrini 2005).

Just how play and recess found their way from community playgrounds into the schools is debatable. One argument holds that playgrounds and play workers may have made their way into school as part of an effort to exert greater control over the developing bodies and minds of the immigrant children (Cavallo 1981). To extend this control more broadly school playgrounds were built to accommodate children's play all year round. Around the same time the kindergarten movement and the use of a playful pedagogy was gaining strength in America (Cavallo 1979). Therefore, it could be argued that recess was a byproduct of the converging playground and kindergarten movements.

Is it possible to implement a playful pedagogy in a standards-driven society?

Those who embrace the concept of childhood as a vital stage of development understand the importance of including time for play and exploration in the lives of children. Some in the field of early childhood education endorse the notion of developmentally appropriate practices that advocate for an "emergent curriculum [that is] sensible, but not predictable. It requires of its practitioners *trust in the power of play*—trust in spontaneous choice-making among many possibilities" (Jones and Nimmo 1994, p. 1). According to Jones and Nimmo, "good programs for young children encourage them to become competent players" (p. 1).

Activity 3

Conduct a classroom observation of an early childhood or elementary school classroom and document the presence or absence of elements on a playful pedagogy spelled out in this section of the chapter (play, playful learning, and playful teaching). Next, reflect on how the presence or absence of these elements impacted the learning environment (student engagement, classroom culture and climate, teacher attitude). In order to conduct such an observation proper permissions and background clearances must be obtained.

For over a century play has been recognized as a vital aspect of learning and healthy child development and so it is surprising that some still question the value of play (Moyles 2010). Some Western nations endorse play-based curricular approaches in early childhood education. For example, the Early Years Foundation Stage (EYFS) curriculum (DfES 2007) in England stresses the value of play for children up to age five. In the Welsh Foundation Phase Curriculum (DCELLS 2008) play is viewed as a key component of children's emotional and intellectual growth. Scotland's new Curriculum for Excellence, early years phase, highlights opportunities for children's engagement in exploratory and spontaneous play (LTS 2009). With these and additional curriculum initiatives around the world (see Kelvin & Lauchlan 2010) early childhood education and play have acquired an elevated status.

Why then do we discourage children from engaging in playful activities at school that are essential to their learning and development? The answer to the question in England stems from initiatives stressing literacy and numeracy requirements that emphasize formal learning, target-setting, and assessment regimes (Adams et al. 2004). Similarly in the United States, federal mandates in the form of National Education Standards, Race to the Top Goals, and Early Learning Challenge Initiatives all emphasize greater school and teacher accountability for adequate yearly progress goals measuring student proficiency in reading and mathematics (Patte 2009). To illustrate, a current report produced in the United States by Miller & Almon (2009) highlights the negative effects of stifling play for kindergarten children, stating: "when children are given a chance to initiate play and exploratory learning, they become highly skilled in the art of self-education and self-regulation … [a play-based approach]is the antithesis of the one-size-fits-all model of education" (p. 5).

In addition, the idea of playful pedagogy suffers from the century-old tradition that teaching is a formal and structured activity. Moyles (2010) suggests that we need to shift our focus from teaching to playful pedagogy and to endorse a wider range of learning and teaching practices to meet the needs of twenty-first century learners. Such a stance requires teachers to rethink some long-established values about schooling and to recognize what children can achieve through play. As the Action Alliance for Children (2007) states, "Play is not a break from the curriculum; play is the best way to implement the curriculum" (p. 2). In the same report it is stated that "research suggests that over-use of didactic teaching can suppress child-initiated learning and undermine young children's self-confidence and motivation to learn" (p. 3), citing Singer et al. (2006) as evidence.

So, to implement a playful pedagogy into a standards-driven curriculum some advocate melding a variety of teaching styles to create a pedagogy of appro-priate practice. For example, Dewey (1916) and Bredekamp & Rosegrant (1995) have identified useful models for understanding the work/play relationship and how it might be actualized in practice. Dewey's continuum identifies five teaching behaviors including fooling—play—work/play—work—drudgery, whereas Bredekamp & Rosegrant's continuum highlight three, non-directive (laissez faire)—mediating (emergent, negotiated)—directive (didactic). Examining both continuums suggests that aspects of both work and play can be infused into an appropriate pedagogy for children that breaks down the age-old "child-centered versus teacher-directed learning" debate.

In reality, teachers have always moved fluidly along a continuum of teaching strategies ranging somewhere between mediation and direct instruction, but today's classrooms are more apt to stifle and discourage child-initiated learning than to support it due to a philosophical shift emphasizing achievement (The Alliance for Childhood 2009). The opinions about the role of play in the classroom are played out through two opposing points of view advocated by learning theorists and child development experts. On one hand, learning theorists advocate a traditional approach emphasizing basic skills that employ teacher-directed instructional approaches like recitation and memorization. On the other hand, child development experts guided by constructivist theories of child development support a child-centered approach stressing child-initiated learning activities. With each aspect of learning and instruction carefully spelled out in comprehensive content standards spanning preschool through high school, Elkind (2007) asserts that it seems almost irrelevant to inquire about the status of play in the modern-day classroom.

Three recent university research studies document the endangered status of child-initiated play in kindergarten classes in New York and California. The two quantitative studies conducted at Long Island University and UCLA surveyed 254 teachers in full-day kindergartens in New York and Los Angeles. A third research team from Sarah Lawrence College conducted a qualitative study by using comprehensive observations in fourteen kindergarten classrooms in New York along with interviews of teachers and administrators. The studies paint an accurate picture of how children spend their time in public kindergartens today. The findings suggest that

- The vast majority of classroom time is devoted to teacher-directed instruction in literacy and numeracy.
- Most of the kindergarten classrooms devote time daily to prepare for and administer standardized assessments.

- Time for daily child-initiated play is limited to thirty minutes or less and in many classes there is no playtime at all.
- The major barriers to play identified by teachers are that the curriculum ignores it, there is no time, and that administrators do not value it.

Both play and pedagogy have many associated terms including free play, free-flow play, spontaneous play, and directed play—just to highlight a few. According to Smidt (2010), play always has purpose to the child even if at times it may appear purposeless to the teachers. Goouch (2008) asserts that playful pedagogies allow teachers and children to interact in playful ways together. During such interactions the teaching style respects and values contributions of the children to their own learning. Within a playful pedagogy the play may be co-created between adults and children with the adult acting as a sensitive co-player. Creativity and innovation are two important components of playful pedagogies as well.

Moyles (2010, pp. 20–2) provides an effective working definition of a playful pedagogy through exploring three important concepts of play and playfulness: (1) play; (2) playful learning; and (3) playful teaching.

1 *Play*—this includes pure play that is controlled by the children. This type of play is initiated, led, sustained, and developed by the children for their own purposes. It represents activities and responses selected and owned by the children and employed at their own discretion. It is highly creative, open-ended, and imaginative. This pure play may only partially be achievable in school settings but is the type of play that links most closely to children's intuitive ways of learning. The role of the adult is to make resources available, to be an interested observer (curriculum and assessment), to interact if invited, and to understand the children's play from a developmental perspective. Such an approach requires a very open-ended planning system by teachers.

2 *Playful learning*—this includes learning experiences that are initiated or inspired by either the child or the adult that engage the child in playful ways and as much as possible reflect the child's instinct to play. It may be led by playful teaching but the child may not consider the activity to be pure play. It is common for children to learn from each other in this context. In this frame the adult has many roles, like being sensitive to playful learning modes, making planned provision, modeling, participating, interacting, enhancing vocabulary, perceiving curriculum and learning intentions within the play, and observing and assessing children's learning needs linked to planning.

3 *Playful teaching*—this includes teaching that draws upon the child's natural and inborn joy for playful learning. It provides that assignments presented to

children as much as possible are open-ended, imaginative, and active. Such teaching employs materials children perceive as playful, but teachers should not expect the child to consider the activities as play. The goal of this teaching must correspond to what the child needs to do in the context of what the teacher wants the child to learn. The teacher's job is to present assignments in an enjoyable manner and to connect with the mandated curriculum and assessment expectations.

These three concepts encapsulate playful pedagogies as they employ a variety of pedagogical strategies from teachers. In practice, the concepts need to be considered both individually and collectively. When reflecting on pedagogical approaches teachers need to consider the number of opportunities in a day or in a week each child has for engaging in these varied pedagogies and plan accordingly. Goouch (2010) argues that perhaps with thoughtful planning children could spend all day in pure play contexts and still fulfill mandated curriculum requirements. Playful learning and teaching offer teachers greater opportunities for engagement in the play of children. When teachers reflect on why they enjoy teaching more playfully, witnessed first-hand by children's increased engagement, it becomes easier to change one's pedagogy (Moyles 2010).

Many scholars recognize the importance of incorporating play in the school environment (Edwards & Brooker 2010; Fromberg & Bergen 2006; Kuschner 2009; Patte 2009; and Sigel 1987).

Example of research:

For example, a longitudinal study by Marcon (2002) of children who began school at age four was conducted to examine the influence of three different preschool models on later school success. These urban children were studied again in year 5 and in year 6 if not previously retained. The study critiqued report card grades, retention rates, and special education placement of 160 children at the end of their fifth year in school and 183 children at the end of their sixth year in school. The sample included 96 per cent African American and 54 per cent female, with 75 per cent of the children qualifying for free or reduced school lunch and 73 per cent living in single-parent families. The girls surpassed boys academically at the end of year 5, and this difference continued into the next grade level. Children who experienced academically directed preschool had been retained less often than peers. No differences attributable to preschool model were found for special education placement. By the end of

⇨

children's fifth year in school, there were no significant differences in academic performance of children who had experienced three different preschool models. By the end of the sixth year in school, children who experienced academically directed preschool earned significantly lower grades compared to children who had attended child-initiated preschool classes. Children's later success in school appears to have been improved by more active, child-initiated early learning experiences. Further, their progress may have been slowed by overly academic preschool experiences that introduced formalized learning experiences too early for most children's developmental status.

In addition, recent research provides evidence that learning takes place through connections made within the brain as a result of external stimuli obtained through the senses (Blakemore & Frith 2005; Geake 2009; Jong et al. 2009). Greenfield (2008) highlights the malleability of the brain in early childhood and worries that the ability of children's brains to make sense of their playful experiences may be compromised by the current emphasis on the fast-paced sensory experiences. According to Moyles (2010) it is clear that there is a major difference between performance (jumping through hoops) and internalization (make learning their own) for children. Internalization requires significant understanding that can only be gained through first-hand, playful experiences.

For example, the complexity of children's pretend play and its connections to early literacy, numeracy, and problem-solving are highlighted by Van Hoorne et al. (2007). Although we still have much to learn about what children learn through their play (Elkind 2008; Broadhead et al. 2010) we can observe the evidence play offers for powerful expressions of understanding, enjoyment, and dispositions to learning.

The findings highlighted here support the idea of playful learning endorsed by contemporary and classic child development scholars (Hirsh-Pasek et al. 2008; Piaget 1962; Vygotsky 1978). Play in a variety of forms, especially those that encourage child-initiated exploration and curiosity, helps to develop knowledge and skills crucial for future academic achievement. As noted by Sigel (1987), rigid learning environments highlighted by high levels of teacher-initiated instruction work against a child's natural curiosity to explore new concepts, which may explain why such environments are not viewed as effective in much of the educational literature.

How can we make the case for child-initiated, unstructured play during the school day?

According to Warner (1877), that traditional bright spot in a school world of discipline and weariness know as recess was alive and well in the schools of New England:

> But recess! Was ever an enjoyment so keen as that with which a boy rushes out of the school-house door for ten minutes of recess? He is like to burst with animal spirits; he runs like a deer; he can nearly fly; and he throws himself into play with entire self-forgetfulness … For ten minutes the world is absolutely his; the weights are taken off, restraints are loosed, and he is master for that brief time … And there is the nooning, a solid hour, in which vast projects can be carried out which have slyly matured during the school hours; expeditions are undertaken, wars are begun between Indians and settlers … or games are carried out on which involve miles of running, and an expenditure of wind sufficient to spell the spelling book through the highest pitch. (pp. 67–8)

All children, like their grownup counterparts, relish a break throughout the course of a hectic school or work day. Primary school children experience such breaks in the form of outdoor recess periods. These school recess periods are recognized cross-culturally as a vital aspect of the school day when children engage in any number of freely chosen activities with their peers without overdue adult intervention. For example, it is common for Chinese and Japanese schools to offer breaks between lessons (Stevenson & Lee 1990). In addition, during this time, preschool children are typically offered a break from the early childhood classroom (Blatchford 1998).

Recess Marginalized

However, despite the positive outcomes associated with recess, a movement is sweeping across the US and UK to reduce and eliminate recess across early childhood, elementary, and middle school education. The trend toward marginalizing recess has been documented by three surveys. The first survey, conducted by the National Association of Elementary School Principals (1989), found that 96 per cent of schools surveyed offered one or two recess periods each day. Just ten years later, a second national survey revealed that only 71 per cent of the sampled kindergarten classrooms had a daily recess period (Pellegrini

2005). A similar trend was observed in a national survey conducted in England (Blatchford & Sumpner 1998) that found a consistent decline of recess time over a five-year period (1990/1991–5/1996). These declines in recess were reported in both elementary schools (56 per cent) and secondary schools (44 per cent).

Example of research:

Recess today has become a lightning rod in an evolving national debate about the role of schools in advancing optimal child development and well-being. Recess has traditionally served as the main outlet throughout the school day where children are able to reenergize their developing bodies and minds. But the time to do so has been eroding steadily with time. Decreasing time devoted to daily recess in favor of increasing time for academic preparation is a growing trend in many schools that began in the late 1980s (Patte 2009). The trend to reduce spontaneous play in US schools was accelerated with the passage of No Child Left Behind in 2001, particularly in urban schools with large numbers of children from underrepresented populations (Pica 2005). For example, Ohanian (2002) found that the urban Atlanta school system built schools without playgrounds to demonstrate their devotion to high academic standards. Further, up to 40 per cent of US elementary schools are reducing or eliminating recess time to prepare for tests (Zygmunt-Fillwalk & Bidello 2005; McKenzie & Kahan 2008). Marano (2008) asserts that some 40,000 schools no longer provide play time for children. In addition to decreasing time devoted to recess for academic reasons, it is also often withheld from students as a punitive measure for any number of indiscretions. Such measures deprive students of many benefits important to their health and well-being (CDC 2008).

Reflections on the research

In the hopes of increasing academic achievement of students, many schools today opt to cut or eliminate time for children to participate in recess. However, recent studies suggest that these efforts may prove to be more harmful than helpful to students. For example, Smith & Lounsbery (2009) found that reducing time for recess and replacing it with more time for academic learning have not realized increases in student achievement. In fact, evidence suggests that opportunities to be physically active, like those offered through recess breaks, are related to higher levels of student attentiveness which correlate with improved academic achievement.

Activity 4

Principle 7 of The Declaration of the Rights of the Child states in part that "the child shall have full opportunity for play and recreation, which should be directed to the same purposes as education; society and the public authorities shall endeavor to promote the enjoyment of this right." Reflecting upon the results of the research studies mentioned above, do recent societal trends seem to support or detract from Principle 7?

Theories supporting the inclusion of recess at school

A rationale to maintain and actually increase opportunities for children to participate in daily recess periods can be based upon two complementary theories. The first is based on the idea of massed versus distributed practice (James 1901). This theory holds that attention to classroom tasks will be maximized when children's efforts are spread out or distributed across time. From this view, learning is maximized when there are breaks in the completion of challenging cognitive tasks. Second, cognitive immaturity theory (Bjorklund 1997) holds that children's developing nervous systems and lack of experiences make it difficult to perform higher-level cognitive tasks as well as older children and adults. Therefore, young children should perform best when there are breaks between intense cognitive activities. The cognitive immaturity theory (Bjorklund & Green 1992) argues that children will be more focused after participating in recess. A recent study offers credence to this argument.

Summary of research

Activity Breaks Improve Academic Performance and Classroom Behavior

The studies highlighted here suggest that regular physical activity breaks during the school day may improve academic performance, academic focus, and classroom behavior.

- In a study conducted by Barros, Silver, & Stein (2009), teachers reported improved classroom behavior for approximately 11,000 8 to 9-year-old students participating in more than 15 minutes of daily recess.
- A survey conducted in 2008 of personnel from 106 school districts in North Carolina found that the most widely cited benefit on a new state policy mandating at least 30 minutes of recess for students in kindergarten through eighth grade was improved academic focus (Everson, Ballard, & Lee 2009).
- Jarrett, Maxwell, & Dickerson (1998) found that a sample of 43 fourth-grade students from Georgia exhibited greater levels of on-task behavior and fewer instances of fidgeting on days with a scheduled activity break compared to days without one.
- A 2006 study by Mahar, Murphy, & Rowe examining the effects of providing an activity break for elementary school children (K–4) found that providing a daily physical activity break improved on task behavior significantly.

Activity 5

Using the information gleaned from the studies mentioned above, prepare an "elevator speech" that advances the benefits of recess to the development of the whole child. An elevator speech is a brief summary used to advocate your case to an influential audience quickly. The idea behind the elevator speech is that it should be possible to persuade your audience to consider your position in the time frame of a typical elevator ride (30 seconds–2 minutes). Consider a variety of audiences who would benefit from this speech. Deliver and refine the speech often.

Interview with Olga Jarrett about her research

Olga Jarrett, Professor, Georgia State University

Michael Patte: **How did you first become interested in studying recess?**
Olga Jarrett: Conducting research on play and the importance of play in the lives of children has been a research interest of mine for a long time. My husband and I had lived overseas in Germany for eight years and our children attended the Department of Defense Schools there where the children participated in daily recess. When we moved back to America and settled into the Alanta area, my son came home after his first day of elementary school and said "Mom, we have no recess". At first I thought that it might be due to a hectic first day schedule, but after a little digging I learned that our school system had abolished recess. This seemed so unreasonable to me and I just could not believe that children were not getting any break throughout the school day. This was the impetus for my advocacy and research interests concerning recess.

Michael Patte: **Please describe some of your research concerning recess that included children in the process.**
Olga Jarrett: This topic proved to be a very interesting topic in my graduate seminars and some of my students invited me into their classrooms to conduct research about the impact of eliminating recess on the well-being of their children. One study I conducted examined recess in a fourth grade departmentalized classroom with two groups of children. We studied both groups and looked at the children's behavior when they had recess and when

they did not have recess. This school did not have daily recess and so we obtained permission to let student have recess several days a week. As part of this study we interviewed the children on what they thought about recess and what they thought about physical education (PE) class. These recess-deprived children brought up that they though recess was a right and that PE class was very different from recess. Although the children enjoyed PE class, they had to do what the teacher told them to just like in any other class. But during recess, the children got to do what they wanted to do. The children also mentioned that they were not able to talk during their lunch period and the noise at lunch was measured with a yacker-tracker (green-yellow-red light) noise monitoring system. They started to speak about their rights as kids and they felt that their rights were being violated.

Another point at which children became involved in the research was through "the problem solution project". This was a required project for university students in one of our programs. The year we were trying to get recess legislation passed through the state of Georgia's Legislature many graduate students focused their energies on saving recess. In fact five class-rooms in the same school building chose recess as the focus of their project. The elementary school teachers collected data out on the playground to determine what the children were doing, how they were using the equipment, etc. After collecting the data the teachers presented their findings to the principal and convinced him to let the children have recess in spite of the fact that offering recess was against board policy. So I think children can play a very important role is serving as strong advocates for recess as it is something they really care about. Due in part to our initial efforts to reinstate recess, the school board policy has been changed to include opportunities for daily recess. Every school district was required to develop a local board policy about recess and report it to the state.

Michael Patte: **I know that you recently conducted a very extensive literature review on all aspects of recess research. What did the current literature reveal?**

Olga Jarrett: Up to about 10 years ago, we found that there was not that much research conducted during recess but quite a bit of brain research suggesting that the brain needs periodic breaks from learning—the kind of breaks that recess supplies. We also found quite a bit of literature focusing on playgrounds, in particular community playgrounds on which children were exploring various types of equipment while developing social skills. There was also some research that found children exhibited more off-task behaviors when deprived of recess. In the last 10 years, many studies have been conducted during recess showing physical and social benefits.

***Michael Patte*: So are you encouraged by the recent studies exploring recess in terms of what they are finding?**

Olga Jarrett: Yes. It is great to have such a wealth of research, but much of it now focuses on activity level. That is important due to the current obesity rates among children in the West. However, there are so many other important aspects of recess to consider as well. In our earlier recess research, children often commented that recess was the only time during the day when they were free to talk with their friends. Another study I conducted in an urban school highlighted the importance of recess and its role in encouraging creativity. During recess these children often tweaked, modified, and morphed various games they learned in physical education class by creating rules, negotiating, and developing leadership skills. Due to high level of engagement among the children, we experienced very little fighting.

I would like to see more longitudinal studies being conducted over the course of a school year that examine the effects of recess on learning. Currently there are a few studies that show children are more on-task after recess or an activity break compared with those lacking such a break. Some current studies are also finding disparities among groups of children who have access to recess. These disparities seem to be based upon ethnicity and socio-economic status.

***Michael Patte*: Why do you see access to play and recess in particular as a human rights issue?**

Olga Jarrett: I think the right to do what the body needs to do is a human right. Keeping children confined to a chair in the classroom for six or seven hours, instructing them to place their hands over their mouths as they walk down the hallway, and prohibiting them from talking during a 20-minute lunch period seems to me to be violating some pretty basic human rights. In my view, children should not be deprived of the opportunities to socialize and move about freely for part of the day and that is exactly what is happening in many schools every day. I am very concerned about the fact that the US has not ratified the Convention on the Rights of the Child. I am often left wondering what rights do children have in this country. Do children really have the right to play? Legally, maybe they do not. Another common practice is for teachers to deprive children of recess time as punishment for bad behavior.

Benefits of recess for the whole child

There are many studies highlighting the multiple benefits of recess on the development of the whole child. As touched on earlier, recess can be thought of as a break from the rigorous cognitive tasks taking place during a school day (Burgeson, Fulton & Spain 2007). Following is an examination of the cognitive, social, emotional, and physical benefits realized when children participate in daily recess periods.

Cognitive benefits

Children are thought to learn best by doing and recess provides opportunities to develop intellectual constructs and cognitive understanding through active, hands-on manipulative experiences. Such exploratory experiences are common in unstructured socially engaging environments like the school playground. During free play, children expand their imagination and creativity, develop and implement their own unique games, create and alter their own rules, learn to develop problem-solving skills, and enhance leadership skills (Bergen 1998; Waite-Stupainsky & Findlay 2001). Further, recess has been shown to improve cognitive focus that helps children to be more productive and attentive in the classroom (Pellegrini 2005; Ginsburg 2007). In fact, the ability of students to refocus cognitively was enhanced more by the break from the classroom than by the type of activity that occurred during the break (Stellino & Sinclair 2008).

Social and emotional benefits

Recess provides fertile ground for enhancing social-emotional learning and growth for children through offering ample time to partake in social interactions and to develop and act out vital social skills (Pellegrini et al. 2002). Play at recess also allows children to develop essential interpersonal skills including cooperation, negotiating, problem-solving, and sharing (Sibley & Etnier 2003). These interactions at recess provide children with the time necessary to adapt and adjust to the multifaceted school environment. Further, being that recess provides a break from the mental rigors of the school day, it offers children a means for managing and relieving stress and for honing other necessary coping skills like perseverance and self-control (Bjorklund & Brown 1998). It is through peer interactions like these that children develop the necessary social skills to interact with peers in a positive and productive manner.

Physical benefits

Daily recess provides many health benefits for children, including enhanced aerobic endurance, muscle strength, motor coordination, and attentiveness. According to Clements and Jarrett (2000), children's bodies experience heightened physical growth between the ages of 4 and 12, and vigorous physical activity during recess stimulates the development of the heart, lungs, and other vital organs. Although not all children play vigorously at recess, it does offer opportunities for children to be active in a mode of their choosing, to practice movement, and to refine motor skills. Even minor movement during recess counteracts the elements of a sedentary lifestyle children experience both at school and at home (Ridgers et al. 2007). Waite-Stupiansky & Findlay (2001) found that children's participation in vigorous physical activity in the schoolyard surpasses that which occurs during more structured physical education classes. Further, the Center for Disease Control and Prevention (2004) reports that regular physical activity is associated with healthier lifestyles and greater life expectancies. In addition, Rivkin (2001) found that most children who play outside on a regular basis are healthier, and physically active children are more likely to become physically active adults.

Summary of research:
The State of Play: Gallup Survey of Principals on School Recess

This poll is the first nationwide, scientific survey of elementary school principals devoted to the study of recess. Administered in October 2009, the survey included 1,951 administrators from a balance of urban, suburban, and rural school across the United States.

Key Findings:

1 Recess has a positive impact on achievement and learning.
   - More than 8 in 10 principals report that recess has a positive impact on academic achievement.
   - Two-thirds of principals report that students listen better after recess and are more focused in class.
2 Recess benefits child development in important, non-academic ways as well.
   - A majority of principals (96 per cent) believe that recess has a positive impact on social development.
   - A majority of principals (97 per cent) believe that recess has a positive impact on general well-being.

3 Recess remains a precious commodity at most schools. Despite its links to achievement, many schools cut recess to meet testing requirements.
- Half of principals report that students receive between 16–30 minutes of recess per day.
- One in five principals indicate that annual yearly progress (AYP) testing requirements have led to a decrease in recess minutes at their school.

4 Despite the connection between recess and good student behavior, schools continue to take recess away as a punishment for bad behavior.
- Most principals (77 per cent) report taking recess away as a punishment.

5 Recess is the time of day when schools face the biggest behavior management challenge.
- Principals report that the majority of discipline-related problems occur outside of class time (87 per cent) with the majority of those occurring during recess or lunch (89 per cent).

6 Schools are looking for help with recess.
- When asked what would improve recess at their schools, principals prioritized a list of items including: an increase in the number of staff to monitor recess, better equipment, and playground management training.

Activities—The following activities are designed to help the reader reflect back on some of the key concepts explored throughout the chapter

Activity 6

The inclusion of play as an important and consistent part of the school day has changed over time.

- How do you view these changes being supported and challenged within the examples of research throughout the chapter?

Activity 7

Moyles (2010) provides a useful framework for instituting a playful pedagogy through infusing three important concepts of play and playfulness into school curricula: (1) play; (2) playful learning; and (3) playful teaching.

- Using examples of research from the chapter, reflect upon the benefits and drawbacks of implementing playful versus didactic instructional practices.

Activity 8

Use the examples of research on recess to answer the following question.

- What does the recent marginalization of school recess say about how society views children?

Summary

This chapter has:

- explored how the role of play in schools has evolved over time.
- examined how to implement a playful pedagogy in a standards-driven society.
- argued for the inclusion of child-initiated, unstructured play during the school day.

Further reading

Barros, R. M., Silver, E. J. & Stein, R. E. K. (2009) School recess and group classroom behavior. *Pediatrics*, 123, 431–6. This is a study examining the amount of recess that children 8 to 9 years of age in the United States receive and compares group classroom behavior of children receiving recess with that of children not receiving daily recess.

KaBOOM (2009) *Play matters: A study of best practices to inform local policy and process in support of children's play*. Washington, DC: Author. The purpose of this report is to describe successful local initiatives to improve opportunities for play and draw conclusions about why they have worked. The impact of these initiatives is gauged across three dimensions: increasing the quality of available play spaces and play opportunities, improving the quality of spaces and experiences, and increasing safe access to play. The report also identifies emerging data linking play initiatives to positive outcomes in health, education, the environment, and the economy.

Marano, H. (2008) *A nation of wimps: The high cost of invasive parenting*. New York: Broadway. This book connects the dots between over-parenting and the social crisis of the young. Psychology expert Hara Marano reveals how parental overinvolvement hinders a child's development socially, emotionally, and neurologically. Hothouse parenting has hit the mainstream—with disastrous effects. Parents are going to great lengths to take the lumps and bumps out of life for their children, but the net effect of parental hyper-concern and scrutiny is to make kids more fragile.

Robert Wood Johnson Foundation (2009) *Active education: Physical education, physical activity, and academic performance*. San Diego, CA: Author. This research brief documents the decline of physical education in the United States due primarily to budget concerns and pressures to improve academic test scores and offers evidence to suggest that children who are physically active and fit tend to perform better academically.

Play and Other Institutional Settings

Introduction and key questions

What comes to mind when you think about the time-honored saying "the best things in life are free"? Chances are that today, the list of things that come to mind might be a bit shorter compared with a list compiled thirty years ago. Did you ever envision children paying to experience the joy of playing on a playground or exploring a wild nature area? The notion of pay to play is a reality for many children throughout the world today. The popularity of commercial playgrounds in countries such as the United States and United Kingdom is on the rise as even the once-sacred realm of children's play becomes commodified. In this light, play is viewed as something to be consumed rather than enjoyed. Sadly, children often play a marginal role in the creation or selection of these play spaces as it appears such playgrounds provide mainly for the needs of adults with respect to how they want their children to play, and to a lesser extent for the children's play needs.

In addition to exploring the controversial phenomenon of pay for play, the chapter also examines how play is experienced across a variety of other institutional settings through answering the following questions.

- Should children be required to pay to play?
- How do children play in hospitals?
- How do children play in prisons?

Activity 1—Debate

Organize a debate on the topic pay for play. One group will take the position that a commercial playground should be built in the local community while a second group will make the case for building a free access playground. Both groups will conduct research on the pros and cons of each playground configuration and present their cases to a third group of students serving as a playground planning panel. After deliberation, the panel will render a decision on which playground to build for the local children.

Should children be required to pay to play?

Pay to play, often referred to as pay for play, is a common phrase used to describe situations where money is paid for the privilege to participate in play or other extracurricular activities. Although a recent trend, many view this practice as a burden to children and families and as an affront to the long-standing tradition of free play provision. For example, the adventure playground movement endorses a concept known as "the three frees" when describing access to play spaces for children. This concept states that access should be *free of charge*, that once admitted children are *free to come and go* as they please, and that children are *free to choose* where they play, how they play, with whom they play, and how long they play (Else 2009). The idea of providing play space for children at no cost is challenged by the commercial playground movement and the practice of charging fees for participation in a variety of extracurricular activities.

In a 2009 practice briefing titled "Developing an adventure playground: The essential elements", Play England defines what is meant by the term adventure playground and sets out what is expected of local authorities charged with designing and developing these play spaces. The briefing defines adventure playgrounds as:

spaces dedicated solely to children's play, where skilled playworkers enable and facilitate the ownership, development, and design of that space—physically, socially, and culturally—by the children playing there. The indoor and outdoor area is enclosed by a boundary which signals that the space within is dedicated to children's play and that activities such as digging, making fires, or building or demolishing dens—activities not normally condoned in other spaces where children play—are provided and encouraged (Play England 2009).

The practice briefing also identifies twelve essential elements of an adventure playground that offer children the widest range of opportunities for play, including:

- Spontaneous free expression of children's drive to play.
- Engagement in the full range of play types as chosen by children.
- Exploration of physical, social, emotional, imaginary, and sensory spaces.
- Free flow is giving and responding to play cues to ensure children can determine the content and intent of their play.
- Creating a shared flexible space that children feel has a sense of magic.
- A rich and evolving indoor and outdoor play environment, where children can play all year round in all weathers.
- The active involvement of children and young people in creating and modifying the play space, within a varied landscape.
- The playground is at the heart of the community.
- The playground is staffed by skilled and appropriately qualified playworkers working to the Playwork Principles (PPSG 2005).
- It is designed to be accessible to all children, and is based on inclusive practice so that disabled, non-disabled children and children from minority communities are welcomed and enabled to play together.
- Entry to the playground is free of charge, children are free to come and go and free to choose how they spend their time when there.
- Risk management is based on the principle of risk-benefit assessment, balancing the potential for harm against the benefits children gain from challenging themselves in their play.

The thing that is so refreshing about adventure playgrounds is that each is its own unique place; it is not possible to prescribe what it should look like or what characteristics it should offer. This philosophy stands in stark contrast to the cookie-cutter fixed structure playgrounds and commercial playgrounds that dominate the play landscape today (Else 2009). All play spaces should enlist participation from the children and local members of the community as a place that children own and are encouraged to shape and develop.

Commercial playgrounds

The popularity and growth of the commercial playground movement is evident in many Western cities, and is attributed to the commercialization of children's play, parental control of where children play, a shift in focus from quantity of play environments to quality of play environments, a reorganization toward private provision for leisure and away from public provision, the practice of transporting children to and from leisure activities, and in part a reaction to the health risks associated with inactive children. However, in a society that glorifies the commodification of childhood, providing access to pay for play seems to be a simple solution to a complex problem.

McKendrick et al. (2000) identified these commercial indoor establishments as play zones that are constituted on the principle of pay for play, or based on one's ability to pay. Recognized by names like Crazy Tykes, Wacky Warehouse, the Mischief Factory, and Funhouse, these spaces of consumption assemble arenas for play, sports, parties, and coffee bars to produce an attractive destination for diverse populations. Advertisements for these commercial playgrounds are filled with propaganda appealing to parents' desire for safety and children's need for excitement. One play zone even states on its website that children who attend will not only have fun, but improve their physical stamina and social competence as well. These play zones further function as community meeting places where parents can sit and relax over a coffee while their children burn off steam at any number of prescribed activities. Although parents and children are often physically separated in these play zones, the rooms are often connected with a variety of electronic surveillance equipment. Children, families, and even schools can occupy these play spaces for hours or days on end as a variety of overnight camps are one of the program choices offered.

Commercial playgrounds encompass a wide range of play environments located primarily in urban centers often in close proximity to shopping precincts (Mintel 2006). Access to these play spaces is based upon a variety of factors including mobility, ability to pay, ability to follow prescribed rules, and that parents take responsibility to ensure that children are obeying these rules. Like many preschools, commercial playgrounds are organized into discrete groups based upon physical characteristics like a child's age or height. Similarly, these play spaces differentiate prices for schools and various groups based upon total time of use or number of times something is used, making them spaces of efficiency.

Most commercial playgrounds include five distinct zones encompassing entry points, functional zones, active play zones, transitional space, and zones of consumption (McKendrick 1999). For practical purposes all commercial playgrounds must have an entry point where patrons expect common services to be offered. Parents concerned about accessing a safe space for children to play find clear points of entry, restricted means of exit, and functional utilities as valuable features of commercial playgrounds (McKendrick 1998). The active play zone is the space set aside for play and is often organized into specific areas for older and younger children. This zone is off limits to most adults except for employees responsible for maintaining the play space. The commercial zone encompasses an area near to the active play zone where refreshments are sold to children and adults. However, this zone is thought of as primarily a space for adults to congregate, socialize, and relax. Finally, there is a transitional space located between the active play zone and the commercial zone that serves as both a site for play and a site between play.

What is the appeal of commercial playgrounds?

There are many societal factors that make these pay for play commercial playgrounds an attractive option for modern-day parents including living in a culture of fear, a lack of freedom to explore outdoors, a tendency of parents to overorganize the lives of their children, and a lack of access to natural spaces.

Example of research

The increase in popularity of supervised, controlled play spaces for children is partly attributable to a rise of parental anxiety for children's safety creating a present-day culture of fear (Gill 2007; Furedi 2002; Marano 2008). These feelings of anxiety are heightened by national media stories documenting child abductions commonly referred to as "stranger danger" cases. Recent survey research suggests that few parents allow their children to play unsupervised and that children commonly identify fear of abduction as their greatest concern about playing outside (Gill 2006). Ironically, statistics suggest that children are safer today than ever as incidences of child abduction and murder are very rare and have remained flat over the past fifty years.

An additional factor drawing parents to commercial playgrounds is a decline in freedom to play outside for children living in both rural and urban communities. Studies examining children's independent mobility suggest that it has decreased to a ninth of what it was just thirty years ago. To highlight, Hillman et al. (1990) suggests that elementary-aged school children have a smaller and more clearly specified play area, are monitored more frequently by parents, and are more likely to have their play interrupted at any sign of foul play. An additional a concern expressed by parents about letting their children play outside is traffic danger. This fear of traffic causes parents to exclude children from the natural habitats in the local community. However, research by Risotto and Giuliani (2006) found that children who walked to school exhibited well-developed spatial skills and a greater knowledge of the social fabric of the neighborhood than those driven to school, demonstrating the importance of navigating streets to cognitive development and community awareness.

Following are some fictitious examples from the research study that highlight specific environmental competence skills.

> "Maria loves cakes. She can always tell you which local cake shop has the freshest whipped cream, the richest cheesecake, the vanilla slice which melts in your mouth or the lightest puff pastry. She also knows which of these shops is nearest to home and which is furthest away, yet she can't explain to her friend, who lives in another part of the town, which of them would be her nearest cake shop."

> "Anna often takes her dog for a walk and she likes to let him wander off the lead. On one of their walks she discovered a car-free track between two rows of houses: an excellent shortcut for walking to school."

> "It's always David who decides where he and his friends will play football in their neighborhood: he not only knows where, but also when to play so that the neighbors don't complain about the noise."

> "Mark stopped wanting to go to school on his own because of a menacing drunk he always encountered on the way. When Louis showed him another route, frequented by more people and with fewer risks, he was very relieved."

These excerpts from the research exhibit the different types of relationships that exist between children and their surrounding environment. This research provides an opportunity to ponder an interesting question: What does knowing your own local surroundings or the environment in which one lives, mean?

A final reason some parents view commercial playgrounds as a viable option for their children is due to a lack of quality local place spaces. In a recent poll, 59 per cent of parents reported that there was no outdoor play space within walking distance from their home; in lower socioeconomic neighborhoods, the number jumped to 69 per cent (KaBOOM 2009).

Reflections on the research

Parental fear of strangers and busy streets as well as access to quality play spaces are common present-day barriers to children's play identified in the various research studies mentioned above. While these fears are very real for parents, the statistics suggest that children are safer today then ever. There is an age-old adage that claims children should be seen and not heard but today such sightings of children are becoming more rare. For example, Penn (2005) highlighted that "one of the most significant changes in the urban landscape over the last century has been the disappearance of children ... Like the skylark they have become endangered" (p.180). So rare is their sighting, that when children do appear in public unsupervised today, they may be viewed as a potential problem. Worse yet, their parents may be viewed as neglectful at worst and irresponsible at best.

Activity 2—Conduct a neighborhood play audit

Walk around your local neighborhood in search of spaces where children can play (streets, parks, gardens, etc.). Next, determine whether or not children actually spend time playing in these spaces. After conducting this informal audit reflect on your findings in light of the societal factors mentioned in the research above that make commercial playgrounds so appealing to may parents today. What are the underlying societal factors causing this apparent disconnect between parent fears and national statistics on child safety?

Fees for participation in school extracurricular activities

A growing trend in schools across the United States requires students to pay fees to participate in extracurricular activities from sports to bands and including school clubs. Recent National data gathered in 2009 sheds some light on the state of pay for play in America. The National Federation of State High School Associations (NFSHA) published the results of a survey that reported thirty-three states in America presently report using pay to play options. A more recent, albeit smaller national sampling conducted by the National Interscholastic Athletic Administrators Association (2010) found that 60 per cent of respondents did not charge fees for participating in interscholastic athletics. Of the 770 respondents representing forty-eight states, 33.5 per cent reported charging fees and either have increased or will increase existing fees in the 2010–11 school year.

The practice of pay to play has been found to be unlawful in some states due to certain provisions establishing a right to a free public education. Due in part to court rulings various interpretations, or statutory prohibition, some states believe extracurricular activities should be considered a vital and necessary component of the public education guaranteed by state law (see in California, Hartzell v. Connell [1984] 35 Cal.3d 899, 201). In these states opponents of pay to play practices argue that the benefits (interpersonal relationships, teambuilding, problem-solving, language development, and reasoning abilities) of participating in these extracurricular activities should be enjoyed by all. Further, some of those opposed to pay for play use the slippery slope argument (PSBA 2010). This argument holds that levying fees for extracurricular activities will eventually lead to charging fees for others as well with the line between what becomes fee-based and what does not becoming blurred at best. As more and more programs become fee-based the potential exists for schools to become stratified by socio-economic status, which many believe is counter to the notion of a free public education.

An additional concern of pay to play policies is their potential impact for smaller programs, sports, and clubs. These vulnerable groups that depend on scant numbers of students for sustainability might cease to exist if students who cannot pay decide not to participate. Research by PSBA (2010) suggests that participation rates of students in pay to play programs do not diminish significantly if fees remain low ($50–$100), but as fees increase to limits reaching ($300), participation can drop as much as 30 per cent. On a related note, critics of pay to play argue that parents who pay fees for the children to play sports may feel entitled to certain amounts of playing time for their children. These parents, paying up to $1,500 in some schools, may have a hard time watching their child sit on the bench, and may have different expectations from students and parents not experiencing a pay to play mentality (PSBA 2010).

However, most states do not fund participating in extracurricular activities as part of a guaranteed basic public education, which leaves the decision to levy such fees to local school officials (PSBA 2010). Advocates of pay to play fees view them as a valid funding source, especially in the current tough economic times. When compared to eliminating activities, cutting core funding streams, or raising local taxes, these fees can be seen as the lesser of two evils. Proponents of these fees further argue that such fees are a more equitable way of funding extras in which only a few students may participate.

Whereas the first part of the chapter explored the emergence of the pay for play movement and its impact on children and families, the next section of the paper explores how children experience play in hospital settings.

How do children play in hospitals?

Each year thousands of children are admitted to hospitals due to a variety of illnesses and injuries. This hospitalization experience provokes high levels of anxiety for both children and families. Common emotions experienced by each include behavioral regression, anxiety, fear, aggression, and apathy (Adams et al. 1991). Hospitalization further exposes children to a variety of significant stressors including invasive exams, limited activity, and separation anxiety (Bossier 1994). Spirito et al. (1994) found that children identified pain as the most stressful aspect of hospitalization. Stressors like these often elicit negative emotions that can adversely impact a child's long-term prognosis (Lepore et al. 1997). In addition, negative emotions have been shown to heighten stimulation of the sympathetic nervous system leading to increased blood pressure and heart rate which can increase a child's overall recovery time (Rozanski & Kubzansky 2005).

The benefits of play in the lives of children are varied and well documented. For example, Jarrett & Maxwell (2000) found that play enhances a wide range of social/emotional competencies including coping skills, self-discipline, aggression control, and conflict resolution. Still others suggest that playfulness and the ability to play promote rapid adaptation to changing environments (Ellis 1987; Fagen 1995; Wickelgren 1993), allow children to psychologically cope with past and present concerns, and prepare us for future roles as adults (Sutton-Smith 1982). While these positive outcomes are beneficial to the well-being of all children, they are especially important to the healing process of sick and hospitalized children (Patte 2010a). Healthcare professionals find that play offers an important coping mechanism for hospitalized children that allows them to process through an illness, a procedure, a surgery, and other invasive treatments. Play also fosters self-expression that allows sick children to openly and freely express a full range of feelings. Such openness allows medical professionals to better understand a child's fears and feelings about a wide range of illnesses.

Example of research

Patte (2010) conducted a study aimed at identifying the therapeutic benefits of play for hospitalized children. In the course of his research he investigated the roles performed by the hospital play specialist. He found that the most common forms of therapeutic play they used to help children cope in hospitalized settings were:

- *Bereavement play*—allows children to express fears and emotions relating to the end of treatment and dying through a variety of activities including memory boxes, hand and footprints, creative and expressive arts, messy play, puppetry, storytelling, and role-play.
- *Developmental support play*—supports normal childhood development that may otherwise be disrupted as a result of hospitalization and treatment.

Examples include peer group activities that allow the young patients to learn social skills.

- *Diagnostic play*—helps to gain insight into a patient's fears and understanding of their illness or treatment.
- *Distraction play*—is based on the premise that the more young patients are absorbed in play and distracted from a medical procedure, the less their experience of pain. It can include the use of bubbles, puppets, music, guided imagery, and other relaxation techniques.
- *Expressive play*—enables young patients who have trouble verbally expressing complex feelings associated with illness, injury, or hospitalization to express feelings and energy in an acceptable, pleasurable, and physical manner. Examples of expressive play include target shooting with syringes, throwing wet sponges, pounding/banging activities, cooking activities, and throwing activities.
- *Medical play*—prepares young patients mentally for painful or invasive procedures through familiarization of the medical equipment and process, and rehearsals of helpful coping behavior. Some common examples of medical play include collages made from medically related materials, band-aid ornaments and necklaces, mobiles created with healthcare-related materials, exploration and manipulation of medical equipment, surgical mask creations, and IV pole decorating.
- *Post-procedural play*—allows children to discuss a treatment or procedure and to work through fears or concerns and reflect on ways to cope during future treatments and procedures.

Reflections on the research

All children benefit from engaging in various forms of play, but these benefits are especially important for hospitalized children. Probably the most important of element of play for hospitalized children is that it provides a distraction from the anxieties, fears, and tensions often associated with hospitalization. Further, role-play has been shown to increase the level of cooperation between patient and caregiver. In addition, hospitals often provide playrooms for children that serve as procedure-free zones where children can escape from the realities of hospital life and regain command through play. Finally, hospitalized children employ play as a means of socialization where through mutual activities children can connect and help each other through difficult hospital procedures.

Activity 3

The therapeutic play types mentioned above help children to cope with a variety of stressors associated with hospitalization. Reflect on how these types of play might be applied to children experiencing fear, trauma, and maltreatment across various settings, cultures, and societies.

Facilitating play in healthcare settings—what is a hospital play specialist?

Some Western societies have specialized fields of study to train individuals to promote and encourage play in the hospital setting. For example, in the United Kingdom, play in hospitals is facilitated by a hospital play specialist (HPS), a field that can be traced back to 1957. These professionals undergo rigorous training in meeting the play needs of hospitalized children. Play specialists hold a level 3 childcare qualification plus a level 4 in hospital play specialism with the Hospital Play Specialist Education Trust. Although the HPS leads playful activities and encourages the use of play as a therapy, they are neither play therapists or play leaders. Rather, working as part of the medical multidisciplinary team hospital play specialists, they:

- Organize daily opportunities for play in a playroom or at the bedside.
- Provide play as a means to achieve developmental goals.
- Assist children in coping with stressors.
- Use play to prepare children for a variety of medical procedures.
- Support siblings and families.
- Assist in clinical judgments via play-based observations.
- Advocate the value of play to other hospital staff.
- Encourage peer group interactions.
- Organize special events.

The specific techniques employed by the HPS will be dependent on a range of influencing factors as children exhibit different levels of development and cognitive ability that are often influenced by injury and illness.

Over the last four decades hospital play specialists have been successful in convincing the medical profession and other professional bodies that play should be an essential component of pediatric care (National Association of Hospital Play Staff 2000). As evidence, new children's hospitals in the UK are designed with playrooms and are staffed with large play departments employing up to forty HPS each. Further, in general hospital settings smaller teams of play personnel work in outpatient clinics, children's units, and adolescent wards.

What is a child life specialist?

In the United States, child life specialists (CLS) help to alleviate stress and anxiety faced by many children and families in a variety of healthcare settings including hospitals, pediatric physician and dental offices, outpatient clinics, and counseling clinics (Brown 2001). Child life specialists are skilled professionals with expertise in assisting children and families overcome challenging life events. Steeped in the teachings of child development and family systems, child life specialists:

- Promote effective coping through play, preparation, education, and self-expression activities.
- Provide emotional support for families.
- Encourage optimum development of children facing a broad range of challenging experiences, particularly those related to healthcare and hospitalization.
- Provide information, support, and guidance to parents, siblings, and other family members.
- Educate caregivers, administrators, and the general public about the needs of children under stress.

The field of child life can be traced back to 1965 and presently there are more than 400 training programs throughout the United States and Canada. There are three components in the credentialing process of a child life specialist that include a minimum of a bachelor's degree in child life or a related field, the successful completion of a 480–600 hour child life internship, and receiving a passing score on the standardized certification assessment. Like their British hospital play specialists counterparts, child life specialists serve as an integral part of a multidisciplinary and family-centered model of care.

Effective child life programs provide developmentally appropriate play, reassuring psychological preparation for various procedures, and assistance in the planning and rehearsing of coping skills through family support and education (Thompson 1989). Due to its familiar nature for children, play is the primary modality of a child life program. Research suggests that play can make traumatic experiences less frightening and more comfortable for children (Thompson 1995). There are plenty of venues for play in child life programs including medical and surgical areas, clinics, emergency rooms, waiting areas, and sibling care centers. Play opportunities are differentiated for various developmental levels including socio-dramatic play for toddlers and games with rules for school-age children and adolescents (Berk 2004). Further, a variety of auxiliary programs like animal therapy, therapeutic clowning, music therapy, and art therapy offer additional supportive activities spanning the gamut of ages of pediatric patients (Kaminski, Pellino, & Wish 2002).

A second important element of a child life program is preparing children for hospitalization, surgeries, doctor visits, and procedures. The process of psychological preparation involves sharing accurate and developmentally appropriate information concerning stressors and strategies for coping with those stressors (Fortunato 2000). According to McDonald (2001), programs such as these drastically reduce emotional anxiety in hospitalized children.

Family support and education is the third important element of child life services. Family involvement is encouraged in patient care due to the positive impact the family plays in the adjustment of children to the healthcare experience (Johnson, Jeppson & Redburn 1992). Due to the fact that anxiety experienced by family members can be transmitted to the children receiving services, child life specialists help family members understand their child's response to treatment and promote parent/child play sessions for comforting their children during various procedures (Solnit 1984). Many similarities can be drawn between how children and families cope with being admitted to a hospital and when visiting a prison. What follows next is an account of how opportunities for play are actualized in prison settings.

How do children play in prisons?

In America, more than one in every 100 adults is incarcerated, according to a report published by *The Pew Charitable Trusts* (2008). Therefore, over 1.5 million children presently have a parent serving a sentence in a state or federal prison (Mumola 2000). These statistics are especially disparate on families of color, with African-American children nine times more likely and Hispanic children three times more likely than white children to have an incarcerated parent. Between the years 1995 and 2005, there was an increase in the number of incarcerated women in the US by 57 per cent compared to 34 per cent for men (Harrison & Beck 2006), 75 per cent of whom were mothers. Sixty-three per cent of federal prisoners and 55 per cent of state prisoners are parents of children under 18 years of age. The average age of children with an incarcerated parent is eight with 22 per cent of the children under the age of five. Finally, 46 per cent of all parents in prison lived with at least one of their children prior to serving their sentence. Given these statistics it is important to develop play-based programs for children visiting parents in prison.

Children with incarcerated parents are often more likely to be incarcerated as adults than other children due to a variety of challenges including financial instability, material hardship, strain on family relationships and structure, residential mobility, increased likelihood of student behavioral and performance problems in school, along with shame and social and institutional stigma (Hairston & Oliver 2007). La Vigne et al. (2005) found that maintaining contact with incarcerated parents improves a child's emotional response to the incarceration and enhances the attachment bonds between child and parent. There are many programs and services for children with incarcerated parents that are promising in addressing various aspects of children's needs. One such program offered in four prisons throughout the UK, called *The Play in Prisons Project*, was created to enhance parent-child relationships through the medium of play and interaction with the goals of reducing negative effects of parental imprisonment, strengthening family ties, and reducing the likelihood of reoffending.

Example of research:

The Importance of Play in the Prison Setting
This research project was an offshoot of the National Children's Bureau Healthier Inside program, an initiative with the goal of improving the health and well-being of young prisoners (between the ages of 15 and 21) and their children. The project ran from 2008–10 and was supported by the Big Lottery Fund. Results from the project suggest that play opportunities for incarcerated parents and their children are beneficial on many levels (National Children's Bureau 2010).

Key Findings

- Play can help to alleviate many of the negative outcomes associated with visiting a prison.
- Accessing opportunities for play in the home and community environment are difficult for children of incarcerated parents.
- When parents and children play together they realize many benefits including opportunities to bond, strengthening relationships and attachments, and fostering positive emotional well-being.
- By learning how to play with their children and the reasons why doing so is important to healthy child development, incarcerated parents are building the foundation for success when returning to their families and communities.
- Through playful interactions with their children while in prison incarcerated parents can reduce feelings of guilt and loneliness and bolster their self-esteem.
- Play has been shown to strengthen relationships between families which in turn can lessen the likelihood of parents re-offending.

Reflections on the research

Although there are prisons that do provide some type of play facility within visiting areas, the quality of such facilities varies greatly across establishments. The worst of these establishments are unstaffed and unwelcoming, while the best facilities include well-equipped play areas with trained playworkers organizing a variety of activities. If children are lucky enough to be visiting a better facility, they can travel freely between the main visiting room where the prisoners are located, and a stimulating and supportive play environment which can make a typically frightening visit a more positive experience for all (Pugh 2004).

Activity 4—Making the Case for Play in Prisons

You are the head of a national charity that funds a yearly project to support and enhance play opportunities for children in your local community. This year there are two finalists for the $100,000 grant. The first finalist's project is to provide play pods filled with loose parts to encourage child-initiated play at several local elementary schools. The second finalist's project is to institute a play in prisons project in the federal prison in your local community for the children of incarcerated parents. After considering both projects your committee is split right down the middle and you are to cast the deciding vote. In your heart you believe the play in prisons project is the most worthy to receive the funds, but you know that local sentiment will favor the school play pod project. Write a press release that outlines your decision to fund the play in prisons project.

The Play in Prisons Project

Play in Prisons (PIP) is an innovative project aimed at supporting children with an incarcerated parent that ran for three years (2008–11) in the South West of England funded by the Big Lottery. Since 2008, *The Play in Prisons Project* (PIP) has sought to strengthen relationships by assisting children to feel safer and less apprehensive while visiting incarcerated parents. The project introduced several new initiatives involving all family members around the concept of play. These initiatives included specialized children's visits, dads-only sessions, baby and toddler sessions, gym visits for prisoners and their children, and table-top play boxes for families to use during domestic visits. Such initiatives helped to enhance parent/child interactions among prisoners and provided opportunities to learn and practice this skill with their children (Medland-Fisher 2011).

Specialized children's visits—These special visits stood in stark contrast to the more normal domestic visits. First, the length of each visit ran between four and five hours and was offered during school holiday breaks. In addition, fewer families attended when compared to general visits in order to provide a more relaxed environment and additional personal space for meaningful family interaction. Next, prisoners were afforded greater freedom to move freely which provided a sense of normalcy for the families and the ability to engage in a natural manner. Finally, during these visits families engaged in a variety of play activities geared to promote conversation, teamwork, and to have fun.

Dads-only sessions—These visits were four hours in length and were offered during school holiday breaks. These sessions focused on a much smaller number of families in comparison to a general visit in order to ensure staff were able to offer individual support to specific fathers and their children during the dads-only sessions. These sessions began with all visitors congregating together in the visitor's hall to allow the children and fathers to be reacquainted as part of their whole family. Next, the family shared a buffet meal together followed by some joint play time. Then, the incarcerated parent and their children were provided with 90 minutes of quality one-on-one time to become reacquainted again. PIP staff supported fathers in need of guidance.

Baby and toddler sessions—These sessions were very similar in form and content to the dads-only sessions with the only difference being the visits targeted children less than four years of age. During these visits the incarcerated parent was able to feed the child, change the child's diaper, read to the child, and rock the child to sleep. This kind of visit allowed parents to take sole responsibility for their young child's needs, often for the first time, which is vital in building and maintaining a strong parent/child bond.

Gym visits—During each visit children and families were able to access the prison gymnasium where a variety of activities suitable for all ages and developmental levels were provided. This unique venue encouraged a variety of play opportunities including gross motor play, rough and tumble play, games with rules, construction play, and dramatic play. The gym offered a natural and familiar environment for parents and children to play together.

Table-top play boxes—This activity sought to enhance the involvement of fathers in their children's play during restrictive visiting times by allowing children to use equipment from the designated play area at tables where prisoners must remain seated. Allowing equipment to be used at the tables enhanced opportunities for quality family time through positive parent/child interaction. The play materials were organized in a variety of themed boxes to suit a variety of ages and interests.

Importance of play workshops—Medland-Fisher (2011) suggests that some incarcerated parents struggle to relate to their children and find it difficult to play with them after being separated for a period of time. These workshops were offered two weeks prior to an event and were created as a tool to help parents understand specific stages of their child's development, the importance of play to healthy child development, and the importance of becoming involved in the play of their children as a means of building positive relationships moving forward. The primary learning objectives to be achieved throughout the workshops included maintaining relationships during the duration of the prison sentence, reflecting on the inmate's role as a father, understanding the importance of play in a child's development, involving children in the process of visiting, and participating in the planning and implementation of activities during the child-centered event.

Project literature—The PIP project produced a variety of helpful literature aimed at both children and prisoners. As a means of helping children feel safe and stress-free, age-appropriate resources were created to provide practical information about what to expect when visiting a prison. For young children a resource titled *My Visit Booklet* explained the experience of visiting a prison using brightly colored pictures and easy-to-read text. Older children received a leaflet titled *Visiting Soon* which offered a step-by-step outline of what to expect during a visit to the prison with an emphasis on various search procedures and the role of drug-sniffing canines. Both resources are mailed to families prior to attending their first prison event. PIP also created two leaflets for incarcerated parents as a means of helping them understand the significance of parent/child interaction and helping them make the most out of visits with their children. An additional resource offered to prisoners is a revised edition of the book *Daddy's Working Away: A Guide to Being a Good Dad in Prison* that focuses on difficult issues facing prisoners who, although away from their children, still want to be competent fathers.

The lines of research supporting *The Play in Prisons Project* (PIP) draw upon using play as a means of reducing stress and coping with the anxiety of parental separation and employing play as a tool for building relationships between parents and their children. Research suggests that play serves as an effective intervention for children experiencing emotional trauma related to divorce, post-traumatic stress disorder, witnessing domestic violence, and dealing with separation and loss (Le Blanc et al. 2001). Further evidence holds that frequent visits with incarcerated parents in non-threatening settings enhance the social, emotional, and cognitive outcomes for their children (Johnson 1995). Finally, enhanced visiting programs provide greater blocks of time for physical and emotional bonding between children and their parents. This is often overlooked during domestic visits in prison.

The children, intact parents, and incarcerated parents all found the PIP program to be successful in making visits less frightening, in strengthening family relationships, and in providing for a smoother transition in rejoining the family upon completion of the prison sentence. Participants identified a variety of PIP elements contributing to the program's success like having the chance to act like a normal family, playing together in age-appropriate ways, and having the ability to move freely within the space provided when playing and interacting with one another.

The Importance of Play in the Prison Setting

Providing play opportunities for incarcerated parents and their children is beneficial on many levels.

- Play can help to alleviate many of the negative outcomes associated with visiting a prison.
- Accessing opportunities for play in the home and community environment are difficult for children of incarcerated parents.
- When parents and children play together they realize many benefits including opportunities to bond, strengthening relationships and attachments, and fostering positive emotional well-being.
- By learning how to play with their children and the reasons why doing so is important to healthy child development, incarcerated parents are building the foundation for success when returning to their families and communities.
- Through playful interactions with their children while in prison incarcerated parents can reduce feelings of guilt and loneliness and bolster their self-esteem.
- Play has been shown to strengthen relationships between families that in turn can lessen the likelihood of parents re-offending.

Activities—The following activities are designed to help the reader reflect back on some of the key concepts explored throughout the chapter

Activity 5

A central theme of children's access to play revolves around the notion of freedom. Such a stance holds that access should be *free of charge*, that children are *free to come and go* as they please, and that children are *free to choose* where they play, how they play, with whom they play, and how long they play (Else 2009). How do you see this issue of freedom being encouraged and challenged within the examples of research throughout the chapter?

Activity 6

Use the examples of research on play in prisons and in hospitals to answer the following questions.

- Do you think the research supports the claim therapeutic play offers an important coping mechanism for hospitalized children that allows them to process through an illness, a procedure, a surgery, and other invasive treatments?
- How do play in prisons projects compromise or support the opportunity to help children to try and make sense of their situation within the reports of the research?

Summary

This chapter has:

- explored whether children should be required to pay for play.
- examined how children play in hospitals.
- considered how children play in prisons.

Further reading

Dell-Clark, C. (2003) *In sickness and in play: Children coping with chronic illness.* New Brunswick, NJ: Rutgers University Press. Cindy Dell Clark tells the stories of children who suffer from two common illnesses that are often underestimated by those not directly touched by them—asthma and diabetes. She describes how play, humor, and other expressive methods, invented by the children themselves, allow families to cope with the pain.

Shaw, R. (1992) *Prisoners' children: What are the issues?* London: Routledge. This text examines the fate of orphans of justice, looks at the provision for children to accompany their mothers to prison and whether it meets the children's needs, considers the role of healthcare and other professionals in the care of these children, and makes recommendations for improvements in the provision of services for families caught up in the criminal justice system.

Play in Informal Settings

Chapter Outline

Introduction and key questions

This chapter focusses on children's play in non-institutional public spaces; the most obvious example being parks and playgrounds, but as Colin Ward (1978, p. 204) tells us, "children play anywhere and everywhere." Therefore, the scope of the chapter goes much wider to include the streets, the woods and even semi "illegal" places such as derelict land and building sites. The chapter draws on a combination of theory and research to address a number of key questions.

- How do we explain children's preference for playing outdoors?
- What is the nature of natural play?
- How and why has outdoor play declined?
- What are the dangers implicit in this decline?

Children's preference for the outdoors

Anyone who has ever worked with small children will know that given the choice of playing indoors or outdoors, the vast majority will choose the outdoors, even when it's cold and wet. The adults who work with them often find this difficult to accept, but most good quality nurseries view the outdoor environment as being just as important as the indoor environment. In such a setting "the natural world will be seen and experienced from season to season giving the children a true understanding and respect of nature" (Rigg Farm 2011).

Why should it be that small children prefer the outdoors? There are several theories about this, largely revolving around the importance of contact with the "elements". These days we know that earth, water, air and fire are not really elements in the modern chemical sense. However, the idea that these so-called "elements" were at the heart of all matter underpinned most scientific thinking until the late middle ages. Indeed many religions and philosophies still hold to a view that these elements reflect the fundamental make-up of all things. Thus human beings have a long history of respect for these four elements, and many authors think there is an explanation of children's play therein. As Hughes (1996, p. 39) says:

> The life sustaining quality and mutability of the elements, giving rise to myths and rituals, make it vital to have an understanding of their nature and significance. They are a source of both fascination and fear to children and adults. Play is the means by which we explore their nature and deal with the fear they generate.

And subsequently:

> Elemental interaction is another crucial experience for the playing child. For as well as bringing children into contact with life-giving materials, like air and water, and through this contact reinforcing the importance to human beings of free and unpolluted access to these essentials, it may also have a deeper significance. (Hughes 2001, p.64)

In that regard Hughes is thinking of Haeckel's (1901) theory of recapitulation, and its subsequent development by first Hall (1904) and then Reaney (1916). In essence the theory suggests that, especially during their early years, children have a deep-seated need to play out the behavior patterns of their ancestors. Reaney (1916) went further in suggesting that these play behaviors represent an evolutionary summary of the various stages of human history (animal, savage, nomad, pastoral, and tribal). If that were the case then we would expect children living in nomadic communities to play very differently from those living in tribal communities. In fact that is not the case, and Reaney's concept has largely been discredited by anthropological studies of children in nomadic, pastoral, and tribal communities, where it appears children play in very similar ways to each other, and also in similar ways to the play of children in industrialized societies. However, the general idea of recapitulative play should not be dismissed merely because its early interpretation was incorrect. Indeed there does seem to be something quite deep-seated in children's interest in digging holes, lighting fires, making dens, and playing games of chase. It is not hard to see the links between these behavior patterns and those of our ancestors.

There can be little doubt that babies coming into the world today are born with a genetic make-up that is far more suited to a disappearing age. After all, biological evolution moves far more slowly than social evolution. Fay et al. (2001) concluded that there has only been one adaptive substitution in the human lineage every 200 years since human divergence from the rest of the primate world. The human socio-cultural world has changed out of all recognition in that time. During the last millennium we have begun to live an indoor existence. However, the principles of Darwinian evolution would suggest throughout human history babies have come into the world genetically equipped for an outdoor life. It is not unreasonable to assume that is still the case. We are yet to understand the effects of the mismatch between biological expectations and social reality, but whatever problems we may face in the future, we should not be surprised in the present if children want to play outside. Nor should we be surprised by their need to interact with nature in all its forms—animal, vegetable, and mineral.

What do children specifically like about outdoor play places? Waters (2011), in a study of experimental play-based activities, called "narrative journeys," describes an innovative approach to working with children, but one rooted in the deeper subconscious minds of the children. The narrative journeys were piloted by the author in his work at the Eden Project, UK. They were used to connect children practically, imaginatively, and socially to the natural world, and thus encourage place-based learning and cultivate ecological literacy. Waters argues that anthropomorphic narratives, which he encourages during his journeys with the children, may help children develop their natural love for the outdoors, by the careful framing of objects, collaborative and social action, and with the support of an environmentally sensitive facilitator.

Example of research:

Castonguay & Jutras (2009) worked with children (7–12 years old) from what the authors describe as a "poor neighbourhood." The children were invited to photograph outdoor places where they liked to go. In follow-up interviews, the children reflected on their photos, and talked about places they liked and didn't like. They were also asked to identify their favorite place. The aims of the study were:

- to determine which outdoor places the children liked, and which factors influenced their preferences.
- to examine how children's favourite places differ from other liked places.
- to establish which outdoor places children dislike, and which factors influenced their negative perceptions.
- to explore variations in children's perceptions according to individual, family and environmental variables.

Thirty-five children were given cameras, and twenty-nine returned them. Twenty-eight children took part in the follow-up interviews—fifteen girls, thirteen boys. The children produced over 600 photographs (between two and twenty-seven per child). The length of interviews depended on the number of photographs a particular child had taken.

Parks and playgrounds were identified as the most liked places, albeit there was not a great difference between their popularity and that of the other four types of setting identified. The places children liked varied according to their age, but were also apparently affected by the number and range of activities available. In connection with this, the authors use Gibson's (1979) concept of "affordances," which refers to the functional properties of an environment. The children in this study revealed the way in which the affordances offered by different environments can imbue play places with a sense of value in children's eyes. Affordances offered by liked environments didn't just include factors that enhance physical activity, such as swings and slides. The children's responses also confirmed the positive impact of outdoor vegetation, such as trees and bushes for games of hide and seek.

The children's favorite places were usually near a friend's house. Children differentiated favorite places from liked places according to the greater number of positive characteristics and activities they offered. In general they identified at least 50 per cent more characteristics and activities in their favourite place than in one of their liked places. There also appears to be a link between the child's assessment of what it was that made their favorite place so good and the affordance given by that place to using elements in a different way to that which appeared to be intended by the adult designer. This confirms one of Brown's (2003b) findings that children gain more excitement and reward from taking control and manipulating playground equipment than they do from merely playing on it. For example, children appear to gain more from climbing up the sliding surface of a slide than from sliding down it.

Castonguay & Jutras (2009) found that both positive and negative features coexist in play places. Interestingly, as well as being the most liked places, parks and playgrounds were also highlighted as the most disliked places. Physical danger and social/emotional insecurity were the most common factors in causing a child to dislike a place, albeit the authors group all this under the slightly misleading sub-heading of "safety threats." Their analysis of children's activities in such places falls largely under four headings: "passing through (29 per cent of activities mentioned), playing with fixed equipment (21 per cent), playing games with rules (14 per cent), and not doing specific activities or any activities (11 per cent)" (p.105); in other words, in most cases the children are talking about either highly structured activities, or no activity at all.

Reflections on the research

In many ways this reflects another of Brown's (2003b) findings, namely that children have a very effective internal radar system that warns them of impending social danger, in the form of conflict with older children, children from another neighborhood, and unsympathetic adults. Brown observed that children playing happily on playground equipment very often moved away from the equipment as soon as they saw another group of children coming through the gates of the park. He argues that this sort of conflict avoidance antenna is probably part of our genetic make-up, and says the most important cultural rule seems to be "avoid the stare of other children" (p. 244).

Activity 1

If you have access to children through your professional working environment, observe them playing in three very different outdoor settings—e.g. a field, a forest, and a fixed equipment playground. Alternatively, think about your own childhood experiences of playing in different settings. Identify which characteristics of the environment have an impact on the nature of the children's play. What types of play predominate in man-made areas? What is the impact of landscape features on children's play? Do you see any evidence of recapitulative play?

Key points:

- Given free choice, children prefer to play outdoors.
- While playing children benefit greatly from interaction with the elements: earth, water, air and fire.
- Children's genetic make-up prepares them for an outdoor life.
- Children clearly enjoy the apparently recapitulative activity of digging holes, lighting fires, making dens and playing games of chase.
- Parks and playgrounds are the most liked and the most disliked places for playing.
- Children favor play places that allow them some degree of control over the environment.
- Children dislike play places where they feel insecure for physical, social, or emotional reasons.

The nature of natural play

The logical conclusion from the preceding section is that children like to play in the outdoors; they favor environments that facilitate manipulation; and they like to feel autonomous. However, they are wary of places where they feel unsafe. The irony is that the same setting that offers excitement may also offer danger, or at least the perception of danger.

Play England, one of the UK's major play sector agencies, has for many years promoted the idea of natural play. Indeed the recent injection of funds aimed at improving play provision in the UK, via the Big Lottery Fund, the Department for Children Schools and Families, and the subsequent Play Builder and Play Pathfinder programs, saw a vast increase in so-called natural play areas. Unfortunately, all too often these consisted of not much more than a dead tree or a couple of boulders. This missed the point, because the great attraction of the natural environment for children is that it can be manipulated. These over-sanitized playgrounds cannot.

Clearly, this is not satisfactory, and Play England was subsequently funded by Natural England to explore the whole concept of "nature play." Play England recognized the folly of trying to define nature play, so they limited themselves to a description:

> Nature play is children exploring and enjoying the natural environment through their freely chosen play. As well as simply enjoying playing outdoors and discovering green spaces near their homes, mature play could include planting and growing vegetables, fruit and flowers; cooking outdoors; playing with the elements or making camps and dens with natural materials.

Nature play can happen anywhere—in a local patch of grass, green space, bit of woodland or park; in an adventure playground or school grounds; in a garden or allotment; at the beach or in and around a stream or pond; or at destination sites like country parks, forests, environmental and wildlife projects. (Conway 2011)

One very positive outcome of this project is the Online Map of play spaces (see www.playengland.org.uk/map - accessed 18 July 2012). The public are invited to identify a play space near to them, and enter the details onto the map. Several thousand have already been added, along with comments and photos. This could be a very useful resource for anyone who is interested in nature play. It is intended to help children and families find green play spaces near home. The overall aim is to build communities of interest around natural places to play.

Another intended outcome picks up on Hillman's suggestion that the outdoor environment should be seen as the "outdoor classroom." If that were the case, it would lead to a range of benefits, including improvements in "self-esteem and self-confidence" (1999, p. 17). For this reason Play England hopes to promote adventure playgrounds as resources for learning outside the classroom, during the school day. Play England is working with Natural Connections on a national demonstration project to share adventure playground and schools mapping data. In so doing they hope to put adventure playgrounds firmly on the radar of the politicians and civil servants.

It may surprise some readers to learn that London is recognized as a very "green" city, with approximately two-thirds of its area being defined as green space or water, and many sites having an abundance of wildlife. The Mayor's Great Outdoors Strategy, the London Plan, seeks to preserve these spaces and also address deficiencies. If we accept that children's interaction with nature is important for their development, and that natural environments aid emotional equilibrium, then their contact with nature in the city is fundamental to their survival. For this reason the London Sustainable Development Commission contracted the well-known childhood consultant Tim Gill to undertake research into ways in which children could be encouraged to re-engage with the natural environment. Children under the age of 12 were taken as the focus for this research.

Example of research:

Gill's (2011) research fits very comfortably with the starting point of this chapter. It sets out a new vision for children's relationship with nature, and maps out an action plan to reintroduce nature into their lives. Gill's work consists of a comprehensive literature review of recent studies. The purpose of Gill's research was to:

- Summarize the benefits experienced by society from increasing the opportunity for children under the age of 12 to experience nature.
- Identify the most successful interventions to encourage regular access to nature amongst children under the age of 12, and make policy recommendations to facilitate this in the mainstream.
- Support the move of current thinking beyond provision of natural spaces, to focus on actual use of natural spaces.
- Develop alternative metrics that may accurately measure access to nature amongst children under the age of 12.

The main findings from the research were:

- In recent decades there has been a decline in the number of under–12s accessing natural spaces on a regular basis to play.
- London is a very "green" city, yet children's experiences of natural places in the capital have been in long-term decline.
- The decline is steeper for children from poorer families and some black and ethnic minority groups. This is having a negative effect on an entire generation, which is growing up severely disconnected from the natural world.

The report recommends that children should be seen as an "indicator species" of the health of a community. Gill suggests the presence of children engaging with nature in the open air should be seen as a measure of the quality of neighborhoods. The author hopes that the report might be seen as a catalyst for collective action to ensure that experience of natural space is part of everyday life for all of London's children.

Reflections on the research

As Gill says, contact with nature can be seen as part of a "balanced diet" of childhood experiences that promote children's healthy development and general well-being. The very fact that this report was commissioned at all is an indicator of the extent to which children's play has become over-sanitized, and adults have become over-protective of their children.

Activity 2

Gill suggests the lives of children should be seen as an indicator of the health of a community. Do you agree? If so, what does it mean when so many of our children live an indoor existence, and outdoor play is increasingly rare. Consider whether you think that might be storing up problems for the future.

Key points:

- A child's favorite play place may also be the one they are most scared of—the two things are not necessarily mutually exclusive.
- Children don't engage with nature as much as they used to.
- There have been a number of attempts to help children reconnect with nature.
- These have often had only superficial success.
- Children's play experiences should be taken as an indicator of the health of a community.

Interview with Tim Gill about his research

Tim Gill, Writer, Independent Researcher and Consultant

Fraser Brown: **Looking back now, what do you remember most about this piece of research?**

Tim Gill: I was determined to make my literature review as systematic and authoritative as possible given the limited time available. This was for two reasons. First, I didn't want to cover the same ground as the numerous published descriptive reviews on children and nature. Second, I wanted to produce something that would be effective in persuading the sceptical and the as-yet unconvinced; especially those involved in public policy decision-making. I was surprised at how hard it was to resist the temptation to cherry-pick papers and filter findings and conclusions; having said that, I am confident of my analysis and results, largely because of the support I gained from having access to independent academic expertise (in effect, I commissioned a form of peer review).

Fraser Brown: **What did you discover about the process of researching during this research?**

Tim Gill: Carrying out the research gave me hands-on experience of the process of carrying out a systematic literature review, and brought home to me the complexity of the kinds of judgment that are needed—for instance, judgments about inclusion/exclusion criteria, relevant interventions or samples of children, and the relative merits of different methodologies.

The project also reinforced my views about the value of quantitative and empirical research in formulating public policy. And it deepened my appreciation of the relationship between empirical research and values and understandings.

On a practical level, the process showed me that gaining access to full versions of papers is crucial, but can be very difficult. This is especially true for people who, like me, are not attached to an academic institution. If I were not working within fairly easy reach of the British Library, I simply would not have been able to complete the review without spending hundreds of pounds on online access.

Fraser Brown: **Did anything surprise you about either what you learnt, or the way the research developed?**
Tim Gill: One novel aspect of my review was that I explored the role of engagement style in connection with children's engagement with nature. I did this by analyzing studies according to whether the style of engagement was playful and child-initiated, or more structured and directed. This was a key question for me at the outset, and while I had a hunch about what might emerge—that more playful styles would be more significant—the strength of that finding was unexpected.

The decline in outdoor play

As long ago as 1990 Hillman et al. (p. 79) stated: "the geographical scope of [children's] play territory has been much reduced, along with the amount of unsupervised time they spend outside the home." Since then, the situation has only become worse. In the modern world, opportunities to play are increasingly limited (Ward 1990; Bateson & Martin 1999; Chilton 2003; Wooley et al. 2009). Therefore, the child's potential for development is restricted. Cunningham & Jones highlight the fact that children are now less able to range freely throughout the environment. In these circumstances, the playground might become "a very valuable and necessary part of the child's opportunity spectrum of play environments" (1999, p. 16). In other words, a facility which used to be a minor factor in the child's play environment, might now have the potential to provide fundamental developmental impetus. In Bateson's (1955) terms, the playground would be changing roles from *text* to *context*, and becoming a key part of the child's life experience. Thus, Cunningham & Jones (1999) are presenting quite an optimistic view of the future of play space.

However, this flies in the face of a great weight of evidence that suggests children do not use playgrounds very much at all (Lees 1970; Becker 1976; Wong 1981; Brown 2003b). This is a phenomenon that applies all over the Western world. For example Churchman & Ginsberg (1981), in a study of children in Israel, found a similar lack of interest in playgrounds. In a comparison with Hillman's (1990) study, O'Brien (2000) identified a further decrease in independent use of public space for ten to eleven-year-olds. More recently Charles & Louv (2009) have confirmed the disparity between children's use of the natural play environment and that of their parents at a similar age. They provide evidence that this problem is taking hold far beyond the UK and USA; for example in Canada, Australia, Germany, Switzerland,

Israel, Japan, and several Scandinavian countries. Given that play is inextricably linked with individual freedom of choice, there is no reason to think children will start to use any specific space just because a group of adults have decided to describe it as play space (Ward 1978). In an article in *Leisure Manager*, a representative of one of the leading equipment manufacturers commented: "It is not very often that you see a couple of ten-year-olds going for a stroll in the park to find the space that has been specially designed for them" (KOMPAN 2001, p. 21). Forty years ago, Littlewood and Sale (1973) found that playgrounds only constitute about 10 per cent of all the areas that children identify as play space. There is no reason to think that may have changed. Areas that please adults do not necessarily attract children—nor are they necessarily high in play value (Brown 2003b). It is not surprising then that traditional playgrounds are fairly unpopular. Children give a wide range of reasons for their reluctance to use playgrounds, including boredom, lack of challenge, bullying, "flashers," dogs, broken glass, etc. (Cunningham & Jones 1987). For many children (not just the older age group) the equipment is seen as "babyish" (Williamson 1985).

Over forty years ago, Holme & Massie (1970, p.191) found that older children could be expected to travel further afield with friends, and further still with parents. They also found that visits to parks and larger playgrounds tended to be with parents. In a more recent study, the Children's Play Council (2002, p. 11) came to the conclusion that "children and young people's use of the outdoors had become increasingly restricted." This confirmed the findings of Bateson and Martin (1999), who are quoted in *Best Play* (NPFA 2000, p.10) saying: "once-normal activities such as roaming about with friends, or even simply walking unescorted to and from school, are becoming increasingly rare."

During the 1980s and 1990s several studies highlighted the changes in children's use of the outdoor environment. In particular there was evidence of parents interfering with children's freedom of movement to an extent not experienced by previous generations. Torell (1990) suggested that, along with distance from the home, and the attractiveness of social networks, children's use of playgrounds is also affected by parental restrictions. Fear of strangers had been fostered by a number of media campaigns, with the result that most young children were playing close to their homes (Parkinson 1987), and only attended playgrounds when accompanied by their parents (Benjamin 1985). In the past it would not have been considered unusual for such children to be found on playgrounds in the care of older siblings. This sort of change to everyday behavior patterns raised issues about the child's ability to play freely, and led to Hillman (1999) expressing concern about both the physical effects and the impact on children's mental health.

It is not just the type and quality of provision, and/or overprotective parents that affect children's range behavior. Gender is also significant. It has been known for many years that girls are far more restricted than boys in their territorial range (Coates & Bussard 1974). In fact, the differences between the play range behavior of boys and girls is quite considerable. Boys follow a similar pattern of progressive detachment from the home environment, but always making their transitional moves at a slightly younger age (Parkinson 1985).

A further factor affecting play range behavior is geography. Rural children travel much greater distances than town children, who in turn travel further than inner city children (Parkinson 1987). However, it should not be inferred that the rural child is more adventurous, or has more exciting play opportunities. The rural play idyll, which was described in so many of Richmal Crompton's (1977) stories about William Brown, is just a story book fantasy. Children who live in rural communities cannot play in the street, as there are no pavements, and traffic tends to be more dangerous where there are fewer speed restrictions. They cannot play in farmers' fields because of pesticides and farm machinery. The woods are in private ownership, protected by wardens and gamekeepers. The result of all this is that rural children often lack social contact with other children (Esslemont & Harrington 1991). This is one of the factors that led McKendrick & Valentine to suggest more research is needed into "the unequal geographies of neighborhood play opportunity throughout Britain" (1997, p. 17).

Much of this evidence is quite dated, but a very recent study by Wooley et al. (2009) shows that the situation outlined by Hillman (1999) has progressed exactly as feared.

Example of research:

In 2009 Wooley et al. produced the "Report to Natural England on Childhood and Nature: A survey on Changing Relationships with Nature across Generations". During one week in March 2009 they conducted an online survey with a sample that was representative of the UK population. The survey engaged 502 adults followed by 502 of their children, together with 648 adults without children. The study was of reported (not measured) use of the natural environment by adults and children. The children were aged 7–11 years old; adults were identified as two groups, aged under 50 and over 51 years of age, in order to explore the possibility of differences between parents and grandparents of the children aged 7–11.

Some of the findings were shocking, revealing the extent to which the lives of children have changed in the last thirty or forty years:

- Children spend less time playing in natural places, such as woodlands, countryside and heaths than they did in previous generations. Fewer than 10 per cent play in such places nowadays, compared to 40 per cent from their parents' generation.
- Three-quarters of adults claim to have had a patch of nature near their homes and over half were there at least once or twice a week. 64 per cent of children are aware of a patch of nature near their homes but fewer than a quarter go there once or twice a week.
- The majority of children (over 70 per cent) say they are supervised wherever they play, albeit only 52 per cent are supervised in the garden and 31 per cent in the streets near their homes. However, this rises to over 80 per cent in natural places.
- Parents would like their children to be able to play in natural spaces unsupervised (85 per cent) but fears of strangers and road safety prevent them from giving much freedom to their children.
- Children would like more freedom to play outside (81 per cent). Nearly half of the children say they are not allowed to play outside unsupervised and nearly a quarter are worried to be out alone.
- Ironically, traditional outdoor activities are as popular now as they were in the past, with all achieving a mean score of 3 out of 5. Building a camp or den and exploring rock pools on the beach were and still are the most popular activities.

There was little difference in attitudes across the country and little difference in attitudes based on whether adults and children live in urban or rural communities.

Example of Research

The findings of the research by Wooley et al. (2009) were confirmed even more recently in the 2011 Playday opinion poll, conducted by OnePoll for Savlon and Play England, amongst 2,000 parents with children under 16 years old in the UK and 2,000 children between the age of 6 and 15. Overall, the survey questions on nature play found that children are missing out on the great outdoors, on the essential childhood experiences that outdoor play brings, when compared with their parents' experiences when they were young. However, ironically both adults and children value outdoor play in natural spaces, with children wishing to play out more and parents wishing them to do so. To summarize the findings:

- As children, three-quarters of adults (72 per cent) spent most of their time playing outdoors—of today's children only 40 per cent of children play outdoors more than indoors.

- 63 per cent of parents would like their children to play outdoors more—59 per cent of children say they would like to play outdoors more.
- Contrary to public perception, the majority of children would prefer to do outdoor activities than play on the computer. Playing at a beach or river (88 per cent), playing in a park (79 per cent), riding a bike (77 per cent), and playing ball games (76 per cent) were far more popular than playing computer games.
- Safety concerns among parents mean that 1 in 4 adults would prefer their child to play on a computer rather than climb a tree, and 1 in 5 would prefer their children to play on a computer than play in fields and farmland.
- There is a decline in play activities that would have been taken for granted by previous generations. 47 per cent of adults say they built a den every week and 38 per cent say it was one of their fondest memories of play when they were young, yet 29 per cent of today's children have never built a den at all.
- Over a quarter of children say they never climb trees—1 in 6 never play in woods and forests, and 1 in 5 never play in fields and farmland. 60 per cent of adults say they played in woods and forests when they were children.
- 42 per cent of children say they have never made a daisy chain, and a quarter say they have never rolled down a hill—a third of children have never played hopscotch and 1 in 10 children have never ridden a bike.
- 67 per cent of parents worry that their children don't have the same opportunities to play outdoors as they did.
- 7 out of 10 parents feel that taking their children to an outside space to play is a real treat and something they do not often do. Children feel the same, with a reported 59 per cent that they wish they could play outside in natural places more.
- Over a third of parents claim their fondest memories of play were making up their own games.
- 1 in 7 parents say they do not know where their nearest natural play space is.

Reflections on the research

In light of all this, it is interesting to reflect on the following account from a first year university student on the BA (Hons) Playwork degree at Leeds Metropolitan University. The students were taken out of the university on a field trip and introduced to a range of popular play activities; after which they were invited to record their thoughts. Here is one such reflective account.

Reflective Account
Mahmuda Khatun—Playwork student

The farm was a new experience for me. I have never helped make a fire before. I really enjoyed that as I've never even seen a fire lit before, let alone helped to light one. I now understand the buzz the children get and why it is so popular. As a child I was not allowed near fire. I suppose the risks weighed up by my parents outweighed the benefits. Now from first-hand experience I see that allowing children to learn from their own experience can only benefit their understanding of the world around them. Seeing the fire flame up, feeling the heat, smelling the fire helps the child learn about the dangers as well as the benefits of fire.

At the farm we were set another task of den building. Den building, along with starting a fire, helps children gain people skills and problem-solving skills, working in a group, taking the best points of everyone's input. Working together in the natural surroundings allows you to engage in play and interaction with natural objects, rather than ones that you should keep neat and clean. It allows you to become adventurous in your environment. The team I was in didn't win, even though I did think the den made by our group deserved the title of best den.

The group returned back to the city, where we were shown three settings where children could come and play in the busy city centre. In contrast to the experience on the farm these places showed how children and young people are greatly let down by the adult perception of how the city should be seen. The settings showed how children were being failed and insulted at the same time. The few provisions for the children in the city centre were very basic and stood out for all the wrong reasons.

Overall the day was an eye-opener to all the beneficial aspects of nature and nature's tools, and how children could risk assess for themselves, and do the same activities as adults without getting hurt. The day also showed how children are being let down in a way that has become accepted by society.

Activity 3

Tim Gill (2007) describes children as a declining species in the great outdoors. He says if these were birds we were talking about, we would be forming a committee to protect them. The findings of Wooley et al. (2009) and the OnePoll (2011) survey have been described as shocking. Do you feel this is a fair description, or are the results merely a reflection of perfectly reasonable changing attitudes towards children and their play? Consider the implications for society in general of a generation of children who have only limited experience of playing outdoors.

Key points:

- The last 30 years has seen a reduction in the use of the outdoor environment as a play space for children.
- Playgrounds are not a popular setting for children's play.
- There are identifiable differences between girls' and boys' use of the outdoors.
- Children roam further afield as they get older.
- Outdoor play is still more popular than computer games.
- Children are prevented from playing outdoors by a range of factors, including parental fears about traffic, strangers, bullying, etc.

The dangers implicit in the decline of outdoor play

There is a great amount of irony in all this. Western societies continue to take away genuinely natural play spaces, to make way for the needs of the motorist. In recent years we have often looked to nature for our inspiration in playground design, but we then take all the nature out of it. We replace the natural spaces with a sanitized version of what was there, but this new version holds little attraction for the children. However, most play provision carries a subconscious message for the child—it's only okay to play in certain designated spaces. In the past children have always played the way they needed to, and made use of the environment to fulfill their needs. Perhaps the modern world is taking away that opportunity.

What is the impact on children's play of children not being allowed out on their own until later in life? What is the impact of there being fewer and fewer opportunities for free play in the outdoor environment? Is it possible that once children are free to range over a wider area, they are already beyond the age where they would want to play in the woods and fields? If so, are we rearing a generation of children who have little understanding of nature and of its developmental potential?

Hall (1904) suggested it would be counterproductive to push a child ahead of its natural stage of development, and Hughes (2003) has taken this idea as a cautionary warning of the dangers of a certain form of play deprivation. He says children are born with a genetic expectation of the type of play they should experience. If that does not happen, they may become very ill as a result. If children are deprived of the opportunity to light fires, stamp on insects, play games of chase, etc., we run the risk that they will grow into adults who still feel the need to enact those forms of behavior (but in a distorted adult mode). Thus, for Hughes, one of the most important roles of the playworker is to recreate environments that allow children to experience fundamentally recapitulative play (see Chapter 6).

Sebba (1991) suggests that children who only experience the indoors are likely to grow up psychologically and physically detached from their environment. As a result, they are likely to develop a negative approach to the outdoor world, rather than a positive and creative one. Thomas & Thompson (2004) say children are losing their natural bond with the environment and that future environmental problems may not be understood as a result.

Wilson (1984) contends that reduced contact with the natural environment will lead to "biophobia" replacing "biophilia." In other words, rather than feeling connected to nature, children will be averse to natural things and prefer man-made environments. Orr (1994) goes further to suggest that this process will result in a brain deficiency in terms of the human potential for creativity and comprehension.

This brings us to the concept of "environmental generational amnesia." Kahn (2002) suggests that during childhood we develop our impression of what constitutes a normal environment. We then use that construction to make judgments about what is an acceptable, or unacceptable, environment once we reach adulthood. With each successive generation the view of what is an acceptable environment changes, and the new generation takes this new state as the norm. He suggests this inter-generational environmental deconstruction will result in long-term physical and psychological harm to society. Pyle (2002) feels this is likely to have a cyclical effect, leading to less variety and more destitute environments. Baxter (2008) links these ideas to Brown's theory of compound flexibility (2003). She says that if we reverse Brown's theoretical cycle and apply Pyle's assumptions, then it follows that the inflexible environment will have a negative effect on the flexibility of the child.

Key points:

- Western societies take away natural play spaces and sometimes offer children "natural" play spaces that have none of the attraction of the real thing.
- We may be rearing a generation that doesn't understand the value of the natural environment.
- The dangers of intergenerational environmental deconstruction are potentially far-reaching.
- Inflexible environments are likely to create inflexible children.

Summary

This chapter has:

- explored the theory that explains children's preference for the outdoors.
- examined the benefits of the natural environment in the play experiences of children.
- analyzed the decline in children's use of the outdoors in their play.

• examined the problems that may arise as a result of the reduction in children interacting with the natural environment while playing.

Further reading

Baxter, N. (2008) Playwork and the environment. In: Brown, F. & Taylor, C. (2008) *Foundations of playwork*. Maidenhead: Open University Press. This contribution to a playwork textbook covers a number of key issues arising from children's use (or increased non-use) of the natural environment. The author explores both the impact of the reduction in outdoor play, and the implications for playworkers.

Gill, T. (2007) *No fear: Growing up in a risk averse society*. London: Gulbenkian Foundation. The author argues that the last thirty years has seen an unfortunate combination of a number of factors (some real, some not so real) that have created a situation where parents are essentially risk-averse. A number of socio-cultural myths are explored, and a plea is made for a move towards more child-friendly communities and a shift in the focus of children's services from protection to resilience.

Staempfli, M. (2009) Reintroducing adventure into children's outdoor play environments. *Environment and Behavior*. Vol.41 No.2, March 2009, 268–80. Over the last decade, awareness about the changing nature of children's play has gradually increased, leading to concerns about a decline in unstructured outdoor play. This article explores the reasons for this change, and proposes adventure playgrounds as a specific type of outdoor play environment that have the potential to offer a wide range of essential developmental opportunities for children.

Play Deprivation

Chapter Outline

Introduction and key questions

In an earlier chapter we looked at the wide-ranging benefits of children's play, and made it clear that those benefits apply both to children's future development, and also to their present state of well-being. Sturrock (2007) has summed this up neatly as the child's "being and becoming." That raises the question, if play is so important in our lives, what are the implications for a child whose freedom to play is restricted in some way? This chapter draws on research from a variety of sources to explore issues relating to play deprivation.

- What is play deprivation?
- How does play deprivation impact on the everyday lives of children?

- What happens to children when they are deprived of all forms of play?
- How does play deprivation relate to other forms of deprivation?
- What are the implications of play deprivation for society in general?

What is play deprivation?

The opposite of play—if redefined in terms which stress its reinforcing optimism and excitement—is not work, it is depression. Players come out of their ludic paradoxes ... with renewed belief in the worthwhileness of merely living. (Sutton-Smith 1999, p. 254)

If Sutton-Smith is correct, then the absence of play from a child's life would indeed be a catastrophe not only for that child, but for their family, and for society as a whole. Clearly the absence of play opportunities, usually termed play deprivation, may take many forms on a spectrum of disadvantage (or neglect, depending on your viewpoint). At one extreme would be the chronic neglect and abuse of abandoned children in Romania during the later years of the Ceausescu era (Webb & Brown 2003), while at the other end of the spectrum, children in modern Western societies may simply be unable to play outdoors because of what Gill (2007) calls their "risk averse society."

The child's right to play

At whatever point on the spectrum the deprivation occurs, in all cases the thing that is being withheld from the child is their freedom to play—a freedom that is enshrined in Article 31 of the United Nations Convention on the Rights of the Child (UNICEF 1991), which states:

1 States parties recognize the right of the child to rest and leisure, to engage in play and recreational activities appropriate to the age of the child and to participate freely in cultural life and the arts.
2 States parties shall respect and promote the right of the child to participate fully in cultural and artistic life and shall encourage the provision of appropriate and equal opportunities for cultural, artistic, recreational and leisure activity.

In any country where the Convention has been ratified, this ought to mean that children can expect to be able to play freely, and that their government should encourage provision for this. In practice that rarely happens, and it may be the case that the right to play freely is the most disregarded right in the whole UN Convention.

Article 31 is not the only part of the UN Convention that has implications for children's play. The following Articles are also relevant to the issue of the child's freedom to play:

- Article 2—guarantees non-discrimination.
- Article 13—guarantees freedom of expression.
- Article 15—guarantees freedom of association.
- Article 19—guarantees protection from abuse or neglect.

The impact of play deprivation

Since the early 1970s, when Suomi & Harlow (1971) summarized their research into attachment and development in a paper entitled *Monkeys Without Play*, we have been aware of the impact of play deprivation. Nowadays their research methods would be considered unacceptable (see Knight 2011 for a wide-ranging discussion of these issues), but that does not mean we should ignore their findings, which clearly indicate the value of play in the early development of infant monkeys. On the basis that monkeys are the closest to homo sapiens of all species on the phylogenetic scale, it is not unreasonable to suggest their conclusion that "monkey play is of overwhelming importance" (1971, p. 491) may also be applied humans.

Example of research:

Harlow's experiments were conducted over three decades between the 1950s and 1970s. In Harlow's laboratory, infant monkeys were raised in a variety of ways. Some were left with the mother and allowed to play with peers. This group showed no developmental differences from monkeys raised in the wild. Others were raised by the mother, but given no peer interaction. These infants developed disturbing patterns of behavior as they matured. Yet another group of infants were isolated from their mothers, but allowed to play with their peers. So long as they also experienced some form of "contact comfort," this group developed normally. The tactile input might be something as simple as a piece of soft cloth, and the play input might be as little as half an hour a day. This led Rosenblum, one of Harlow's collaborators, to suggest: "there are three variables to love—touch, motion, and play—and if you can supply all of those, you are meeting a primate's needs" (Slater 2004).

However, Harlow's experiments did not stop there. A further group of infant monkeys were raised in cages where they were able to see and hear other monkeys, but not able to play with them, or interact in any meaningful way. Not surprisingly in such circumstances, the monkeys developed clear signs of disturbed behavior. Harlow concluded:

> Having no mother or peers to cling to, these monkeys embrace their own bodies in intensive self-clasping. Having no maternal nipple to suckle, they suck and chew their own digits … Having no playmates to provide motor stimulation, wire-cage reared infants develop compulsive and stereotypic rocking behaviors, strikingly reminiscent of the human autistic child. (Suomi & Harlow 1971, p.492)

When Harlow's infants reached physiological maturity they were "incompetent in virtually every aspect of monkey social activity" (1971, p. 492). For example, they showed little understanding of social rules or social hierarchy, often preferring to sit in a corner by themselves, and sometimes engaging in self-harm. Harlow found that when his infant monkeys were introduced to peers, they did not seem able to play. Rather, they avoided social interaction and instead focused on introverted self-satisfying, sometimes self-abusive behaviors. He therefore concluded "no play makes for a very socially disturbed monkey" (1971, p. 492).

Surprisingly, in contrast to all the evidence of social and physical damage, Harlow found that total isolation had "little apparent effect on the monkey's intellectual capabilities" (1971, p.493), a finding confirmed by Brown & Webb's (2005) research in Romania thirty years later.

As a general rule, however, Harlow showed that isolation had a severely damaging impact on an infant monkey's chances of maturing into a stable functioning adult. In stark contrast, when these young monkeys were able to play with their peers for brief periods during their otherwise isolated existence, they developed into normal, healthy, well-balanced juveniles. Consequently, Harlow and his collaborators suggested that play, or the absence of play, was an absolutely critical factor in this process. A little play in the developing years and the ill-effects of isolation appeared to be negated. The final sentence of their 1971 article is particularly relevant here:

> Then pity the monkeys who are not permitted to play, and pray that all children will always be allowed to play. (1971, p. 495)

Reflections on the research

The methods used by Harlow and his team were often brutal and some would say bordering on sadistic. There is clearly no place in modern scientific research for such approaches, which would be considered unethical today. However, the outcomes of these experiments have been instrumental in changing the way we rear children. Harlow proved the importance of love and close physical contact in the early years, with the result that it is now quite unusual to hear any child specialist recommending that mothers distance themselves from their baby. Harlow proved the importance of play in the development of infants, and this is a concept that now pervades most early years' settings, albeit often with greater emphasis on the learning side than the play.

Harlow's experiments were with baby and infant monkeys. Is it correct to say, as he did, that his conclusions can be applied to humans? The general characteristics of children's play are so reminiscent of monkey play that there cannot be much doubt about this. More recent research by Brown & Webb (2005) appears to confirm the parallels. Harlow speaks of the way in which, having no playmates to provide motor stimulation, wire-cage reared infants develop compulsive and stereotypical rocking behavior. Brown and Webb identified an identical pattern of behavior in the Romanian group. Clearly no play makes for a very socially disturbed child. Harlow suggests that damaged infant monkeys may be rescued by placing them in contact with baby monkeys. This is another finding that was confirmed in the Romanian study.

Finally it is interesting to reflect on Harlow's finding that the intellectual capacities of his monkeys were unaffected by their isolation. Once placed in an environment where they experienced cognitive challenge they proved equal to the task. On the face of it, that is surprising. Why would the cognitive processes remain intact when all other aspects of development were so severely affected? It has often been suggested that the cognitive aspects of the brain are not fully switched on until around the age of six or seven (Montessori 1912; Piaget 1962), and in recent years neuro-science has confirmed this (Sunderland 2006). Perhaps the cognitive aspects of the brain didn't get badly damaged in these experiments because they were never substantially engaged. Is it possible that for a bodily function to be badly damaged it has to be operational in the first place? For example, the growth function is operational from birth, but needs children to play in order for them to exercise their muscles. Without play, the normal functioning of the musculoskeletal system will be adversely affected. The brain's cognitive system, on the other hand, simply waits to be switched on by the right sort of stimulation.

Activity 1

It is interesting to reflect on the ethics of Harlow's experiments. Do you think it is ever acceptable to experiment with animals in order to learn lessons for human society? What do you think can be learnt about children's play from watching animal play behavior? What can you definitely NOT learn about children's play from watching animal play behavior? What are the clear differences between human and animal play?

Defining play deprivation

Many writers have highlighted the complexity of play, and the array of different types of play. For example Sutton-Smith (1997) identified seven "rhetorics" within which he grouped 308 different types of play. Hughes (2002; 2006) proposes a grouping of sixteen play types. The significance of this is that, for Hughes (2003), children need to experience the full range of play types during their childhood in order to attain and maintain a state of well-being. Where children fail to do this they may be said to be suffering from a play deficit, and are likely to experience lasting damage. He suggests that the causes of this damage take two quite distinct forms, either play deprivation or play bias. Hughes (2003, p. 68) explains these two concepts as follows:

- *Play deprivation* is the result of either "a chronic lack of sensory interaction with the world," or "a neurotic, erratic interaction."
- *Play bias* refers to "a loading of play in one area of experience or another, having the effect of excluding the child from some parts of the total play experience."

Hughes suggests that deprivation and bias in children's play are far more widespread than society acknowledges, and far more damaging. This is the result of a number of factors, including fear of traffic, perceived stranger danger, parental fears of children engaging in risky activity, etc. This "risk averse society" (Gill 2007) is a theme that will be taken up in the next section.

Key points:

- The opposite of play is not work … it's depression.
- Children have a right to play enshrined in statute, but it is too often ignored.
- If children cannot play it is dangerous for the child and for society as a whole.
- There is a human deficit condition caused by the absence of play opportunities.
- The deficit condition takes two distinct forms: play deprivation and play bias.
- Play deprivation is more widespread than generally thought.
- Play deprivation occurs over a spectrum of disadvantage from mild to chronic.

Play deprivation in the life of today's child

In his excellent text *No fear: Growing up in a risk averse society*, Gill (2007) speaks of the "shrinking horizons of childhood" (2007, p. 12). He reminds us of the findings of Hillman's (1990) study—namely that in 1971 eight out of ten children went to school unaccompanied; by 1990 that figure had fallen to one in ten. Hillman reported again in 1999 to the effect that the situation had now become worse. Gill (2007) goes on to lay out a range of familiar changes that have taken place in the last thirty years, all of which have had a considerable impact on children's freedom to play. He also examines the culprits—the factors that have produced the "risk averse society" of his title. These include:

- A general lack of understanding that risks can be intrinsically beneficial.
- A fear of litigation on the part of those who should be providing play facilities.
- The disproportionate sums of money spent on safety surfacing for children's playgrounds, at the expense of more and better play equipment.
- Stories about anti-social behavior exaggerated in the media.
- The redefining of bullying to include teasing.
- Excessive child protection measures that have the effect of reducing the number of volunteers prepared to run after-school activities for children.
- Parental fear of strangers, exacerbated by media stories about paedophiles.
- Fear of the internet, exacerbated because children are so much more competent at using modern technology than their parents.

When all this is added to the very real increase in traffic on our streets, it is clear that the opportunities for children to explore their neighborhood in free-ranging play activity are becoming more and more restricted.

At the end of the last century Hughes (2000) reported on a study of a geographical area that had all these problems and more. In certain areas of Northern Ireland children were living in a virtual war zone.

Example of research:

The previous subsection mentioned Hughes's summary of the twin concepts of play deprivation and play bias. Here we focus on the lessons to be drawn from Hughes's award-winning[1] study of children's play in urban Belfast during the period of "The Troubles".

Hughes conducted structured interviews with people between the ages of 9 and 54, living in inner-city Belfast. He asked about their early, middle, and late (if appropriate) childhood experiences. Respondents were invited to talk about:

- Games they played.
- Toys and other resources used.
- Their ranging behavior.
- Their freedom of action.
- Their choice of friends.

On the basis of those interviews Hughes concluded that play had been "adulterated." Adulteration is the term Hughes (2000, p.13) uses to describe the "negative impact of adults on children's play." He found four main effects on play:

1 Deprivation and substitution of play types.
2 Saturation by adulterating images and events.
3 Range, choice, and mastery deprivation.
4 Traumatic violation of the play process.

Hughes suggests four damaging outcomes from all this:

- The adulteration of social play fostered the continued propagation of sectarianism.
- The militaristic nature of the child's environmental experience encouraged the adoption of an extremely limited range of play narratives.
- Restrictions on children's range behavior created mental mapping deficits.
- The stress, trauma, and play deprivation of everyday life resulted in neuro-chemical and neurophysiological mutation of the brain.

Reflections on the research

Hughes (2000, p.58) refers to the work of Harlow (see above) and Einon et al. (1978) in suggesting that "symptoms from play deprivation in other species can be significantly reduced when the subjects are given the opportunity to play again." He, therefore proposes a role for playworkers in alleviating the ill effects of play deprivation, but suggests they would need specialist training in the effects of conflict on play. This is a theme that will be taken up later in this chapter, and also in Chapter 6 of this book.

Activity 2

Interview your parents or someone from an older generation to find out about their play when they were children:

- The physical range of their play.
- The extent of their freedom to choose their own play activity.
- The risks they took in their play.
- The presence of adults in their play environments.

Compare their responses to your own experiences of play as a child.

Key points:

- Today's children don't have the same freedom of movement that was enjoyed by earlier generations.
- In risk-averse societies children's play opportunities will be severely restricted.
- Growing up in a society where violence is the norm will encourage children to engage in dysfunctional play.
- Adulterated play is likely to lead to neuroses in later life.

Interview with Bob Hughes about his research

Bob Hughes, Director, Play Education

Fraser Brown: **Looking back now, what do you remember most about this piece of research?**

Bob Hughes:

- How difficult it was to turn data into conclusions.
- Fear—I had to go into some pretty hairy situations alone.
- Feeling very disquietened when I began to realize the extent to which the Troubles had permeated children's lives.
- How incredibly helpful people (including paramilitaries) were.

Fraser Brown: **How do you see the research in relation to your work in less stressful settings?**

Bob Hughes:

- It provides an extreme view of how toxic not playing is to human children, and helps me in calibrating play deprivation's more and less severe affects.
- Preparation is all.
- People seem willing to relate their experiences irrespective of how bad they may have been.

Fraser Brown: **What did you discover about the process of conducting interviews with different age groups during this research?**

Bob Hughes:

- This is difficult. With some people it had to be covert; with another (who was still traumatized) I had to take it very slowly and gently; with another (a child) I began to realize, because of what he was saying, that his father had weapons in the house.
- Perhaps from a research point of view, the main issue was how long the interview should be, and how directive should I be—in other words, what kind of interview was it that I was conducting.

Fraser Brown: **Did anything surprise you about either what you heard, or the way the research developed?**

Bob Hughes:

- I was surprised about how co-opting the material was. I found myself experiencing what I imagined might have been many of the emotions others may have felt for real. I was particularly shocked by the revelation of SPNs, and the likely need of those affected to take control of their situation, which in turn might result in them attempting to assassinate someone further down the line.
- As you can imagine there was a lot of material about explosions, gun fights, riots, and so on. I found it quite difficult by the end not to feel a high level of anxiety on behalf of the speaker. Perhaps I had a sensitivity to this kind of projection. It's something I would need to be aware of in the future.

Author's note: a follow-up question, for the sake of clarification, revealed that SPNs are Stereotypical Play Narratives: i.e. the false narratives children adopt when they feel under the power or control of adults.

The consequences of complete deprivation of play

In most countries it is unusual to find institutionalized abuse of children. Sadly there will always be cases where individual children are systematically abused by those responsible for their care. Such cases are well documented, and tend to fill the front pages of our newspapers for a while. A cynic might suggest that one of the reasons for the media's interest in such cases is their very rarity. However, in the early 1990s the Western world was faced with child abuse on a scale not seen before on our TV screens. In the aftermath of the overthrow of Ceausescu in Romania it became apparent that there were more than one hundred thousand children living in children's homes in the country. The reasons for this are too complicated to explore here. Suffice it to say that large numbers of these children were suffering from horrendous neglect, and in many cases were enduring institutionalized abuse. This was play deprivation on a grand scale. The following research study was conducted right in the middle of this horror.

Example of research:

Research by Brown & Webb (2005) focussed on the impact of a playwork project on a group of abandoned children living in a ward of a Romanian pediatric hospital. Their research study, which contains numerous parallels with the Harlow studies (see above), focussed on the children's subsequent play development. The children, ranging in age from one to ten years old, had suffered chronic neglect and abuse. They had spent most of their lives tied in a cot; they were poorly fed and their nappies were rarely changed. Although able to see and hear other children, they were unable to leave their cots, and therefore experienced little in the way of social interaction.

The therapeutic playwork project began in the summer of 1999 and continues today, albeit in a much reduced form. It started as a result of the concern of the newly appointed Director of the Sighisoara Hospitals, Dr. Cornel Puscas. Although neither a pediatrician nor a psychologist, when confronted with a ward full of disturbed children sitting rocking in their own solitary worlds, he was reminded of one of the most powerful conclusions from the studies of Suomi & Harlow (1971, p.493): "play is of utmost importance for the subsequent social well-being of the individual and those around him." In common with most Romanian institutions at that time the hospital had no spare money. So, hoping to help the children recover, he set aside a room to be used as a "playroom" and approached the UK charity White Rose Initiative[1]for funding to employ someone to play with the children. WRI employed Edit Bus as the first Romanian playworker, and brought her to Leeds Metropolitan University for a specially designed training course. Upon her return to Romania, Edit worked with the children for four months by herself, before being joined by Sophie Webb for an extended period, and later by Fraser Brown for briefer periods. Towards the end of the first year, WRI expanded the staff team to four Romanian playworkers.

In the early days of the project the playworkers had to untie the children in the morning, bathe them, change their nappies, and feed them properly, before taking them to the playroom. They then worked with the children all day, bathing, changing, and feeding them as and when necessary, and enabling them to begin the long road to recovery through play. At the end of each day, the children were returned to their hospital ward. As soon as the playworkers left the hospital, the nurses went into the ward and tied the children to their cots for the night. This daily pattern continued for at least the first year of the project. No amount of pleading or persuasion could change the nurses' behavior.

When children are deprived of play, the consequences are catastrophic. The emotions of this group of children were in turmoil. When the project started they just stared vacantly into space, rocking to and fro in that rolling motion so familiar to anyone who has worked in a mental institution. They generally looked several years younger than their actual age. For example, the team worked with a ten-year-old boy (complete with nappy) who could have passed for a toddler in any UK nursery. The children's gross motor skills were poorly developed, and they possessed hardly any fine motor skills at all. They were incapable of meaningful social interaction, and showed few signs of cognitive functioning. In the first few months the slightest disturbance was deeply frightening, and resulted in a return to the rocking motion.

The following diary extract, which was written after Sophie Webb's first visit to the hospital, illustrates the point:

> *The silence:* Every room was full of children in cots, but it was so quiet. Even when we entered the room there was no sound from the children. They just looked at us. The smell of urine in every room was almost unbearable.

> *The emptiness:* Each room had just the cots with plastic mattresses. The children were dirty and wearing clothes that were too big for them. Some were wearing jumpers as trousers, and none of them were wearing shoes. There were rags around their waists, which I later found out were ripped-up sheets tied to keep the nappies in place. These rags were also used to tie the children to the cots. Most children were sitting rocking and others were standing up banging the sides of their cots against the walls. Giving the children a cuddle was strange as they either held on too tightly, or they remained stiff and unfeeling.

> When I observed the children in the playroom, they were unaware of each other, fixed on their own activities—barely communicating. Some just sat and seemed bewildered and vacant. (Reflective Diary 6th February 2000)

In the early days of the project it was hard for the team to assess which children had been born with a disability, and which were merely suffering from years of neglect and abuse. However, those distinctions quickly became apparent as the children began to develop. Although every child made progress, some forged ahead at such a rapid rate that it forced the researchers to question their own assumptions about attachment theory, the long-term impact of abuse, and the "ages and stages" view of child development. The change in the children's demeanour and behavior resulted in thirteen of the original sixteen being either adopted or fostered within Romania—something that would have been unlikely in the extreme at the beginning of the project.

The children's play development was assessed using an instrument developed for a previous study (Brown 2003b). During a period when nothing changed in their lives, other than their introduction to the playwork project, the children themselves changed dramatically. Their social interaction became more complex; physical activity showed a distinct move from gross to fine motor skills; the children's understanding of the world around them was improved; and they began to play in highly creative ways. They no longer sat rocking, staring vacantly into space. Instead they became fully engaged active human beings. Brown & Webb's conclusion was simple, but striking: the children's developmental progress was clearly identifiable, and apparently made possible through their experience of the playwork project.

The following extract was written towards the end of Webb's first period of working at the hospital, after the project had been running for around six months.

Considering these were the same children who had been tied to their cots, rocking and staring into space only a few months previously, it illustrates the vast change that had taken place in a very short period of time.

> The thing I'm going to miss most of all is coming into the room in the morning. Sometimes Carol or Ion are still sleeping, and it's lovely to be there when they open their eyes. When we open the door there are lots of shouts of happiness and excitement, jumping up and down in their cots. The noise only starts when we open the door, or when they see us through the window—they are so quiet before that. The first thing I do is go around saying good morning to each one and untie them from their cots and get them on the floor. There are lots of morning cuddles. (Reflective Diary 29th March 2000)

In less than a year, these chronically abused and neglected children made the sort of progress that many experts assumed would be impossible. During the period of the research study the only change in the children's life experience was the playwork project. Therefore, it is sensible to ask what it is about playwork that has contributed to these changes. This is a topic that we will return to later in the book.

Thankfully the hospital's approach to the children changed dramatically after about eighteen months. Today all children are treated the same, no matter what their reason for being in hospital. They are bathed regularly, properly fed, and their developmental needs are addressed. Staff turnover saw some of the worst offenders move on, but I am convinced the major causal factor was the example provided by the WRI playworkers who were encouraged to treat the children with love and respect at all times.

Reflections on the research

In the early stages of this project, the parallels between the children in this study and the monkeys in Harlow's study were clear.

- Both lived their lives behind bars (caged monkeys; children tied in their cots).
- Both were raised in conditions where they could see their peers, but were not able to play with them, or interact in any meaningful way.
- Both exhibited compulsive and stereotypic rocking and weaving behaviors, as well as an avoidance of eye contact, and staring into the distance.
- Both engaged in self-harm.
- When first in a playroom, both rejected close contact with their peers.
- In the playroom both showed a lack of understanding of social rules.
- In the playroom both exhibited erratic unpredictable behavior.
- Both appeared to have unimpaired cognitive abilities, except where there was other evidence of birth defects.
- Both showed benefit from the interaction with an infant going through the early stages of development.

Activity 3

Examine the evidence of this study carefully. Consider the following points:

- How do the findings summarized above challenge your ideas about what you think of as basic conditions for children? Try to be specific about which details of the findings challenge your ideas and why that is.
- How does the presence or absence of play and the conditions for play feature in your ideas about basic conditions for children?
- In what ways do the findings challenge our generally accepted view of child development?
- To what extent is it legitimate for the researchers to claim that play was the most significant causal factor in the change of the Romanian children? What supports this claim? What do you think might challenge this claim?

Key points:

- We still hear of cases of abuse and neglect concerning individual children, and sometimes rogue staff in a children's home are exposed in the media.
- Post-war Europe has not seen anything on the scale of the institutionalized abuse of children that took place in Romania in the 1980s and 1990s.
- Contained within that abuse was widespread play deprivation.
- There is some doubt about the "ages and stages" view of child development when it comes to the recovery of abused children.
- There are clear parallels between the Romanian study and the earlier experiments conducted by Harlow and his team.
- Play appears to be a powerful therapeutic instrument in the caring professions' armory.

Play deprivation and other forms of disadvantage

It is generally assumed by well-meaning play providers that poverty and play deprivation go hand in hand. As a result, large sums of money have been spent by both local authorities and voluntary groups installing play equipment (of sometimes dubious value) in the most disadvantaged areas of the country. The UK Government's Play Pathfinders Programme is a case in point. Thirty authorities were chosen as "pathfinders," not for reasons of play deprivation, but rather on the strength of criteria that related largely to social and economic disadvantage, via a needs analysis.

However, it is not clear whether the connection between play deprivation and other forms of disadvantage is really that significant. There may be some truth in the idea that wealthier parents are more likely to take their children to after-school activities, but that doesn't necessarily address the full complexity of play, and only amounts to a couple of hours per week in most cases. What of the child's need to engage with nature as part of their play; to explore their environment; to experiment with their own creativity; to experience freedom from parental supervision, etc.—in short, all the things that make up a well-rounded play experience? There have been very few studies that address this issue. One of the few such studies focusses on some of the poorest, most seriously disadvantaged children in Europe, namely the Roma children of Transylvania.

Example of research:

The focus of Brown's (2012) study was to examine in depth the phenomenon of play within one of these small communities. The study opens with a quotation from his research diary, which neatly sums up the themes of the research:

> Here I am, in a Transylvanian Roma village, wondering whether the poverty of the environment affects the play behavior of the children. These are the most materially deprived children in Europe. Most of them live in over-crowded homes made from mud and wood, with no running water, power, or sanitation. The only toys are those donated by charities, or scrounged from the skips around the nearby town. The children have no personal possessions at all. What they have is shared with everyone else, not so much in a spirit of community, but rather because there is no way of keeping anything private.

> Why, then, are these children the happiest you're ever likely to meet? Maybe it's because they're free to play wherever, and with whatever, they want. Maybe it's because they're playing with close friends and relations. Maybe it's something to do with the strength of their common culture. Maybe it's the wonderful sunny weather. Whatever the cause may be, the energy and enjoyment of the children's play is there for all to see. Sadly, the exuberant joy of the summer months is in stark contrast to the misery of the winter, when temperatures can fall as low as −25°C, and children die from disease and malnutrition.

> (Diary Extract 5th August 2009)

Brown undertook the study because, having worked with the children over many years, he had become increasingly aware that despite their material deprivation, they could not really be described as play-deprived. In fact their play is extremely social and highly creative. Naturalistic observations took place during the summer of 2009, and totalled around 100 hours. Approximately 200 children between the ages of 7 and 14 live in the village at the heart of this study—albeit there is no census information to confirm the exact population. It was not possible to give an accurate figure of how many children were observed during the study—somewhere in excess of 150.

At first sight the mass of data gained during the study appeared quite chaotic. However, careful application of a thematic analysis approach (Howitt & Cramer 2007) revealed a number of themes, which were then used to bring some coherence to the findings. The themes identified were:

- The children played everywhere and with anything.
- There was widespread engagement with the environment.
- There were a great many examples of the children's creativity.
- The theory of loose parts (Nicholson 1971) was much in evidence.
- The children engaged in a great deal of boisterous physical activity.
- Semi-organized games were a regular feature.
- The girls in particular spent a lot of time engaged in chanting games.

The study provides numerous examples to illustrate these themes. Here is a small sample:

- An old bicycle tyre was bowled along like a hoop, and subsequently used as hula-hoop. Eventually it was discarded, and later claimed by two children who twisted it into a figure of eight around themselves. Then they hopped down a hill, eventually tumbling into a heap at the bottom. Despite the cuts and bruises they repeated this at least a dozen times.
- Fertilizer sacks helped create a competition—not by hopping along in the sack like a traditional sack race, but with the sack covering the head, while negotiating an obstacle course. Later the sacks were used to collect nettles, presumably for soup.
- Grass was tied up as a sheaf, with one end whipped tightly. When tossed into the air the whipped end naturally made the whole thing fall to earth like an arrow. This was also used as the touch mechanism in a game of chase—the sheaf being thrown by the chaser.
- A large piece of polystyrene foam was used as a goal post, but blew away when the wind rose. It was also used to model a face.
- The lid from a tin of paint substituted quite well for a Frisbee in a game of Frisbee football.
- A plastic bottle with a string tied around the neck made a musical noise (sort of) when swung round. Alternatively the string was held in one hand, while the bottle was kicked away from the player. On another occasion the string was tied fairly tightly round a telegraph pole. Flat nails were hammered in a circle around the pole to stop the string from slipping down. The bottle was then used like a "swing ball", but played with feet, rather than a racquet. This didn't work very well, but certainly illustrated the creativity of the players.

This study provides a substantial snapshot of the play behaviors in the village during one brief period. Although it is not strictly possible to generalize, it is nevertheless likely that these behavior patterns would be found in most Transylvanian Roma villages during the summer months. It has to be acknowledged that life is very different for these children in the winter, when temperatures can drop to as low as minus 20° centigrade (minus 4° Fahrenheit). The majority of these children are living in abject poverty, in overcrowded houses made from mud and wood, with no running water, no sanitation, and a poor diet. Indeed, Brown reports that during one of his charity's hot food sessions, when the temperature stood at minus 16°C, one little boy arrived wearing nothing but a vest (see: www.arccharity.org). In these circumstances it is not surprising that the infant mortality rate in these Roma communities is around 4 per cent. Clearly these children are very poor indeed.

But what does all this tell us about the connection, or otherwise, between poverty and play deprivation? The children were clearly free to explore and experiment, and the resulting creativity was often impressive. Whether or not their problem-solving skills were enhanced is unclear, and would probably justify further study. The breadth and depth of their social networks were expanded during their playing. There was a great deal of physical activity, with its attendant benefits in terms of motor skills development. This amount of freely chosen interaction with the environment must inevitably lead to cognitive stimulation. The children, through their interaction with a range of playmates, and their imaginative use of the variety of loose parts available in the village, were very obviously engaged in elements of self-discovery. On balance these materially deprived children, who are very needy in so many ways, appear to enjoy a well-rounded play experience.

Reflections on the research

These are among the poorest, most disadvantaged children in Europe, and yet their play is rich in many of the most fundamental aspects of a healthy play experience, albeit there are health and safety issues associated for children who play on rubbish tips. On the basis of this study alone it would be reasonable to conclude that the link between poverty and play deprivation is tenuous at best. However, this study was conducted during the summer, and it is likely that the quality of the children's play is somewhat diminished during the long cold winter months. Perhaps a similar study conducted during that period of the year would go some way towards providing a clearer answer.

Activity 4

- What do you think this research reveals about the relationship between poverty and play? Would you, for example, conclude that (a) it indicates that poverty acts to reduce play, or (b) the link between poverty and play deprivation is tenuous at best?
- This study was conducted during the summer; do you think that has any effect on the research findings? Is it, for example, likely that the quality of children's play living in such conditions is diminished during the long cold winter months?
- Consider the research and its implications for play: is it possible for us to justify spending money on play provision in the poorer areas of our city?

> **Key points:**
> - Play providers tend to assume there is a link between play deprivation and other forms of disadvantage, especially poverty.
> - There is some doubt whether that connection really exists.

Play deprivation: the implications for society

Since the early days of psychoanalysis, and subsequent attachment theory, a link has been made between childhood experiences and the later disturbed behavior patterns of adults. For example, in a study of the characters and home life of juvenile thieves, John Bowlby (1944) was able to identify a history of early prolonged separation of the children from their mothers, and extensive mistreatment by their care-givers. He described these juveniles as affectionless detached children. In an earlier work Bowlby's mentor, Melanie Klein (the originator of psychoanalytic play therapy) had suggested that a child's early relationship with the mother was likely to become a pattern repeated in later life. In *The Psychoanalysis of Children*, Klein (1932) was the first person to suggest that play might be used as a therapeutic technique to help children come to terms with their neuroses and psychoses.

More recently Brown & Lomax (1969), in their study of young murderers, looked at the link between play and neuroses in a different way—namely, play as a causal factor. Their study was prompted by Brown's earlier involvement in the case of the notorious murderer, Charles Whitman. In 1966 Whitman, an apparently "normal" person, went into the tower overlooking the campus of the University of Texas, Austin, from where he shot and killed seventeen people, wounding a further forty-one. Stuart Brown compiled the behavioral data for the team charged with the task of searching for the causes in Whitman's life. That team of experts came from a number of different specialist fields, and the idea was for them to reach a consensus view on the reasons for Whitman's actions. Their conclusions were stark, but nevertheless significant for any study of play deprivation:

> A lifelong lack of play deprived him of opportunities to view life with optimism, test alternatives, or learn the social skills that, as part of spontaneous play,

> prepare individuals to cope with life stress. The committee concluded that lack of play was a key factor in Whitman's homicidal actions—if he had experienced regular moments of spontaneous play during his life, they believed he would have developed the skill, flexibility, and strength to cope with the stressful situations without violence. (Nifp 2011)

Subsequently Brown has studied people from all walks of life, from murderers to Nobel Prize winners, mapping their "play histories." In the case of the murderers in Texas prisons he found "the absence of play in their childhood was as important as any other single factor in predicting their crimes" (Brown 2009, p. 26). On the more positive side he also found that abused children, with a tendency towards anti-social behavior, could have that behavior modified through play.

Clearly many of Brown's studies are of extremely disturbed people, and we are certainly not suggesting here that every child who has their play restricted will develop into a mass murderer. Nevertheless, these studies should definitely encourage us to think deeply about the potential impact of play deprivation on individuals and on wider society. Perhaps our society's general lack of respect for the child's right to play would be tempered if policy-makers realized the dangers associated with play deprivation. The widespread play deprivation identified by Hughes (2003) is a relatively recent phenomenon. As yet, we don't really know what the long-term effects will be. However, we have plenty of evidence of the effect of extreme play deprivation on individuals, and it is not unreasonable to think that slightly milder forms of play deprivation will nevertheless have a negative impact on the general social psyche of Western societies.

Summary

This chapter has highlighted the following points:

- Play deprivation may be viewed as a spectrum of play deficit.
- The child's right to play is enshrined in law, but that right is often ignored.
- It is possible for a child to recover from the ill effects of play deprivation.
- It is not clear whether there is a connection between play deprivation and other forms of disadvantage.
- Society ignores play deprivation at its peril.

Further reading

Blum, D. (2002) *Love at Goon Park: Harry Harlow and the science of affection*. Cambridge MA: Perseus Publishing. In the middle of the last century many psychologists had come to believe that affection was unimportant in the experiences of the developing infant. The work of the scientists at Goon Park changed all that. Under the guidance of Harry Harlow, the group undertook experiments with baby monkeys that proved the importance of love and affection in child development. In this biography Blum offers an insight into Harlow, and also into the work of the group as a whole.

Panksepp, J. (1998) *Affective neuroscience: the foundations of human and animal emotions*. Oxford: Oxford University Press. Panksepp makes the argument that all mammals have a range of fundamental emotions, and that humans can learn much from a study of the neurobiology of animals. There are sections on many forms of emotion, including arousal, pleasure, fear systems, rage, and anger, but the book also addresses a form of emotion not often included in scientific texts—namely playfulness.

Winnicott, D. W. (1971) *Playing and Reality*. London: Tavistock/Routledge. This classic psychology text focusses on the importance of nurturing creativity in young children, and the way in which that will give them the opportunity of enjoying a rich and rewarding cultural life.

Notes

1 Bob Hughes was awarded the Mike Taylor Memorial Prize for Originality and Innovation in Professional Scholarship.
2 For further details, contact White Rose Initiative: The Flying Ferret, 95 Huddersfield Road, Shelley, Huddersfield HD8 8HF.

Part 3
Implications for Children's Lives

Playwork 6

Introduction and key questions

In previous chapters we have addressed a number of issues, identified by research into the lives of children in many societies, that are having a detrimental impact on children's opportunities to play. In particular we have highlighted the fact that "free play" is being seriously curtailed. Of course, many types of play are still available to children, especially the more structured forms, such as games and sports. As we have seen, children are often encouraged to join organized clubs, where they can experience extensive activity programs. However, none of this can be described as free play of the type outlined by Bruce (2011) or Nachmanovitch (1990).

We have also explored the implications for children's rights, especially the right to play as detailed in Article 31 of the United Nations Convention on the

Rights of the Child (UNICEF 1991). We will now focus on a particular way of addressing those issues, an approach to working with children that is popular in the United Kingdom—namely playwork. This chapter draws on the theory and practice of playwork to address a number of key questions.

- What is playwork?
- What is the playwork view of play?
- How does the playwork approach work in practice?
- What are the benefits of the playwork approach?
- How might we analyze the impact of particular playwork settings?

Some parts of this chapter are taken from an article that first appeared in the *Journal of Student Wellbeing* (Brown & Patte 2010)

What is playwork?

Having its roots in the Danish junk playground concept (Sorensen 1947), playwork has developed considerably since the 1940s. It now encompasses everything from after-school clubs to play centres and therapeutic work. Today there are projects pursuing the playwork philosophy in many countries throughout the world, including Japan, Germany, Romania, and most of Scandinavia. On occasions the provision is more structured than would normally be the case with playwork provision in the UK—for example, the playrooms that appeared during the Balkan conflict (Cunningham et al. 2001). Nevertheless, all these projects are seeking the same outcome: namely improved play opportunities for the children they serve.

In the UK playwork has its own qualification routes, ranging from single subject training sessions all the way through to undergraduate and postgraduate degree courses. The latest figures available suggest there are more than 15,000 playwork settings in the UK, around a half of which are after-school clubs. They employ over 50,000 staff, the majority of these jobs being part-time, with women outnumbering men by a proportion of around 7 to 1. After-school clubs provide more than a quarter of a million places for children (SkillsActive 2010). The UK has several non-governmental organizations dedicated to providing support for the playwork profession, including one for each of the home nations. The most successful is probably Play Wales, an organization that managed to persuade the Welsh Assembly Government to adopt a play policy that takes a rights-based approach to policy-making for children (Greenaway 2008). This was the first national government in the world to adopt such an approach.

The playwork profession in the UK takes it as a basic tenet that children learn and develop while they play, and also believes that children need to have access to good quality play opportunities for that process to work effectively. In many societies today such opportunities are sadly lacking. Playwork is substantially about providing those missing opportunities. It has been defined in simple terms as "the specific act of affecting the 'whole environment' with the deliberate intention of improving opportunities for play" (Playboard 1984). It is widely accepted within the profession that playworkers work to a fairly unique value system.

Hughes (1996, pp. 22–3) summarizes the values of playwork thus:

- Trust the child.
- Children's interactions with one another are essentially non-competitive.
- The content and intent of its play is determined by the child.
- Children are whole environment citizens.
- Children are independent beings with human rights.
- Children are lone organisms.
- Children are individuals deserving of respect.
- Playwork is child-empowering.
- Playwork and equal opportunity are inseparable.

In the book *Playwork: Theory and Practice* (Brown 2003, p.52) playwork was described as "a mechanism for redressing aspects of developmental imbalance caused by a deficit of play opportunities." It follows, therefore, that the playwork approach is well suited to addressing the societal factors that are having a detrimental impact on children's opportunities to play in so many Western countries—those factors that have been detailed in the preceding chapters.

From the end of World War II until the mid 1980s the majority of playwork in the UK was focussed on adventure playgrounds—a setting where "children's freedom to come and go as they please was seen as important," and where they were "free to explore their capacity for doing things themselves (e.g. building dens, water and mud play areas, large towers, swings and climbing apparatus)" (Chilton 2003, p. 116). Since then, with the growth of after-school clubs, there has been a clear shift in the focus. Some would say there has been a dilution of the original philosophy—a philosophy that is best reflected in Else's "Three Frees" criteria (2009, p. 157):

1 Provision should be *free* of charge.
2 Activities should be *freely* chosen by the children.
3 The children should be *free* to leave when they wish.

If we accept these criteria, most after-school clubs would not be seen as providing a playwork environment. After all, most children attending such clubs are being charged, and are expected to stay within the club until collected by a parent or carer. To make matters worse, in many after-school clubs the children are presented with a program of activities, so they don't even get the chance to choose how they want to play.

However, it would be wrong to dismiss all after-school clubs on that basis. There are many examples of clubs where the philosophy of "fun, freedom and flexibility" (Brown 2003c, p.54) is to the fore. In such venues children can explore, investigate, and experiment; they can experience risk and challenge; they are able to test boundaries; and often exercise power and control. None of this is made impossible by the fact that an adult is paying a fee, nor that there is a time limit on attendance.

Example of research:

Davidson & Barry (2003), in a study for the Scottish Executive, assessed the benefits and costs of out-of-school care. They identified over a thousand out-of-school care services, providing places for more than 45,000 children. Their aims included:

- The development of an assessment framework setting out the full range of potential social and economic benefits and outcomes of out-of-school care.
- A critical review of research evidence on the benefits of out-of-school care.
- A synthesis of available evidence concerning labor market impacts.
- An assessment of the cost of provision of out-of-school care.

It is clear from these aims that the priorities of the Scottish Executive were not those of playwork.
  The study identified a number of methodological issues, including:

- The problem of identifying the true impact of out-of-school care vis-à-vis the impact of other factors such as family, school, and the environment.
- A lack of longitudinal studies of out-of-school care provision.

Nevertheless, the researchers found much of interest in relation to play and social interaction. They were able to identify improvements in children's life skills and social skills. They suggested that because out-of-school care provides a wide range of activities—everything from free play to supervised homework sessions—the children's levels of achievement are raised above what might otherwise be expected. This is especially important in deprived areas. They also highlighted the importance of a safe and secure environment, which allowed a comfortable mixing of ages, ethnic groups, and children with additional needs. This is especially valuable for "only" children and those from rural areas.

Overall, they say good quality out-of-school provision leads to benefits for not only the children but also the wider community. Benefits include:

- Increased confidence, self-esteem and motivation on the part of children.
- Children's experiences and skills are broadened.
- Curriculum enrichment.
- Health benefits, through healthy eating and physical activity.
- Consultation opportunities with children.
- Development of citizenship in children.
- Alternative activities which counteract anti-social behavior.
- Social inclusion of families, especially from disadvantaged areas.
- Linkages between families, schools, and the wider community.

Finally, Davidson & Barry identify the most important variables affecting the quality of any particular out-of-school care service. First they say we have to accept the fact that most out-of-school provision is not economically viable. That leads them to highlight the importance of government subsidies, whether in the form of grants or perhaps tax breaks.

Reflections on the research

Despite the fact that this research was commissioned partly as a cost-benefit analysis of play projects, the researchers managed to identify a number of factors that might lead to good quality play provision. Perhaps more significant for the playwork profession however, Davidson & Barry found benefits in both the short and long term for individual children. They were also able to highlight a number of very substantial benefits for the wider community. This is a theme taken up later in this chapter when reviewing the research of Maureen Palmer (2008).

Activity 1

Locate an after-school club in your neighborhood. Spend at least two sessions doing voluntary work with the children. Try to identify hard evidence of some of the short and long-term benefits found by Davidson & Barry. Setting these benefits against the costs of the agency, how might such provision be justified?

Key points:

- Playwork is a profession that is well established in the UK.
- Playwork has distinctive assumptions and values.
- The origins of playwork lie in the adventure playground movement, with its "Three Frees" philosophy.
- More recently playwork has expanded to include after-school clubs, so long as they are adopting the "fun, freedom and flexibility" approach.
- The benefits of good quality supervised play provision are far-reaching, ranging from child development to wider community development.

The playwork view of play

It has been argued by Hughes that playworkers have their own distinctive view of play. In *Play Environments: a Question of Quality* (1996, pp.17–20), he gives us a summary of that playwork view:

- Play is freely chosen.
- Play is personally directed.
- Play is intrinsically motivated.
- Play is non-goal directed.
- Play is multi-faceted.
- Play helps children to calibrate themselves.
- Play helps children to contextualize themselves.
- Play enables the creative use of the environment.
- Play is non-detrimental and non-competitive.
- Play helps children to exorcize negative and extreme experiences.
- Play helps adaptation, the use of tools, problem-solving and socialization.
- Play is spontaneous.
- Risk is an essential ingredient of play.
- Play is irrevocably linked to human development:
  - physical/motor development.
  - communication development.
  - aesthetic development.
  - social development.
  - flexibility.

The playwork view of play is outlined more recently in the Playwork Principles, a set of eight statements that seek to identify the unique nature of the playwork approach with regard to working with children.

1 All children and young people need to play. The impulse to play is innate. Play is a biological, psychological, and social necessity, and is fundamental to the healthy development and well-being of individuals and communities.
2 Play is a process that is freely chosen, personally directed, and intrinsically motivated. That is, children and young people determine and control the content and intent of their play, by following their own instincts, ideas, and interests, in their own way for their own reasons.
(PPSG 2005)

It is of course arguable that some of these statements don't stand up to close scrutiny. For example, play is not always freely chosen, nor personally directed, and it often has a clearly identifiable goal. Nor do children always control the content of their play. However, there is no need to delve deeper into the finer points of defining play in this chapter (see Brown 2008, pp.123–7, for a deeper discussion of these issues), because both Hughes and the Playwork Principles are actually highlighting those characteristics of play that are of concern to the playworker. Suffice it to say that playworkers seek to encourage the sort of play that is "freely chosen, personally directed and intrinsically motivated" because it is the opportunities for that sort of play that are being eroded in many Western societies.

The Play Wales website (2011) describes play that has those characteristics as being "a fundamental and integral part of healthy development," and there is a growing body of evidence to support such a view (Panksepp 2004; Pellis & Pellis 2009). Sunderland (2006, p. 104) tells us that "physical interactive play … has natural anti-stress effects, and because it releases opiods it promotes powerful emotional states … helping children to manage their feelings better." Nowadays there is very little debate about the immense benefit of play, but what should we do when play is restricted or biased or deprived altogether? That is where playwork has a role. Playwork is primarily concerned with providing environments that enable children to play freely.

It appears that children have very similar hopes for their experience of a playwork project. Manwaring (2006) found they wanted playworkers who would:

• Provide a wide choice and variety of things to do.
• Allow children freedom and control of what they do.

- Respond to cues to join in with their play.
- Support them in personal challenges.
- Have knowledge of first aid.
- Have good cooking skills.
- Know the structure of the play setting in terms of practicalities so children felt comfortable with any rules.
- Treat everyone fairly and discipline bullying.
- Be understanding and keep things confidential.
- Make them feel cared for.
- Be patient, calm and not easily angered.
- Be inclusive and help children to be inclusive with each other.

Example of research:

The Venture is an adventure playground sited in the middle of one of the most deprived estates in Wales, Caia Park in Wrexham. Hundreds of open access play projects have come and gone during the last thirty years, and now there are only about 180 adventure playgrounds left in the UK. However, in that time The Venture has moved from strength to strength, and is now one of the most respected projects of its type anywhere in the UK. It was used as the model for the program of integrated children's centres in Wales, wherein one of the four key aspects was open access play (Welsh Assembly 2003). A similar process has been adopted in Scotland. The former Secretary of State for Wales, Peter Hain described The Venture as "one of the best in the country, if not in Europe" (St Co Deb 2003). How has this project managed to survive, and even expand, where so many others have failed? One of the explanations lies in the way in which the playworkers relate to the children and the local community.

Brown's (2007) case study of The Venture explored its history, the political battles, and the creative manipulation of funding streams, but also addressed the relationships engendered by a specific way of working with children. Brown explores the degree to which the success story is the result of one individual's skill at overcoming political and financial obstacles (the long-standing manager, Malcolm King). He suggests that is only part of the story, and concludes that the success of this project is also the result of a firm and ongoing commitment to the traditional values of playwork. This modus operandi was summed up by Brown in another publication:

> A good adventure playground empowers its users by offering freedom of choice
> in a stimulating and empathetic setting, with the result that children constantly
> create and recreate their own play environment. (Brown 2003c, p. 59)

Another outcome of this approach was suggested by Malcolm King when he said that in the adventure play setting strong relationships between adult and child are not just possible, but inevitable. That was one of his main aims when he started the project. Not only would the project offer a suitable setting for working with youngsters who had been referred by Social Services, but an adventure playground might also be expected to help their younger brothers and sisters, by "heading them off at the pass," before they got into trouble. Over the years various funding agencies have been especially attracted to the preventive aspects of the adventure play approach, albeit playworkers themselves have often wanted to play down that aspect of their work.

Funding for The Venture has come from a wide range of sources, for a variety of reasons: the Borough Council, who provided three staff and the building, was interested in play and leisure; Social Services, who provided two staff, were interested in addressing issues such as deprivation, social need, and juvenile crime; the early Job Creation and STEP schemes, which provided four staff, were interested in improving the skills and employability of unemployed people from the local area. This broad-based array of values and goals has resulted in a substantial degree of funding stability over the last thirty years.

However, Brown (2007) found that reliable funding was not the only factor. The project is sited in one of the most disadvantaged estates in Wales, and yet it has suffered little in the way of vandalism or theft. The core philosophy of the project and the day-to-day practice of its staff are key factors in its continued survival. All those involved accept that play provides the best vehicle for a child's growth. Play is the child's fundamental tool for exploring the world, their environment, their interpersonal and physical relationships, and their sense of self. Give children a safe, staffed, open access play environment and they will not be able to resist the temptation to play. It is assumed at The Venture that children are biologically predisposed to playing, and once they start, their whole life is affected. The most fundamental lesson from practice is that play works.

So what is it about the environment and culture of The Venture that has led to its continued success? What are the fundamental values and principles that underpin the work? Brown summarizes them as:

- Adopting a child-centred approach.
- Being non-judgmental, non-stigmatizing.
- Never giving up on anyone—always offering a second chance.
- Being aware of, and trying to avoid, "adulteration".
- Employing home-grown staff.
- Nurturing ownership by enabling children to create their own play space.
- Targeting and responding to the most challenging children and young people.
- Providing a broad range of engaging activities to counterbalance ills in their lives.
- Accepting that children's and young people's inclusion is of paramount importance.
- Promoting positive reinforcement rather than criticism.
- Reflective analytic practice.

Brown's case study contains several detailed reflections, largely provided by Ben Tawil, one of the playworkers on the site. They serve to illustrate some of the points/issues raised in the preceding paragraphs. Here is one example:

⇨

The Tree House: There is one tree at The Venture that is suitable for making tree houses. I have never known any children to play in the tree house for more than a week once their version of the tree house has been finished, and I have never known any children to be more than moderately disgruntled about the fact that someone comes along to destroy their efforts. This is another testament to the fact that the process really is more important than the product (Bruce 1994). However I have had to console many a member of staff that has played a supporting role in the process as adults often become very product-orientated, and the sudden loss of a tree house can be very upsetting for a member of staff who may have spent the last week partially reliving their own childhood experiences.

Reflections on the research

This case study outlines the complex nature of reasons for the survival, or otherwise, of playwork provision. It highlights the role of specific individuals, and also of the local community. It shows the importance of developing and maintaining the right contacts, in order to make your lobbying effective. It also reinforces the value of being true to your original objectives. Only by so doing will the local community come to trust the project and its playworkers.

Activity 2

Playworkers see risk and challenge as essential elements of a good quality play environment. Given the modern concerns of health and safety, and our increasingly litigious society, how realistic is it to expect the adventure playground concept to survive in the twenty-first century? Reflecting on the example of The Venture, prepare evidence in support of the adventure playground concept.

Key points:

- Playworkers have their own distinctive view of play as being freely chosen, personally directed, and intrinsically motivated.
- Playwork has its own philosophical tenets: the Playwork Principles.
- The prime focus of playwork is to provide environments that enable children to play freely.
- Funding agencies tend to be attracted to the preventive aspects of playwork, while playworkers themselves are far more interested in the positive outcomes for individual children.
- Playwork works best when it is child-centered, non-directive, non-judgmental, avoids adulteration, cedes control to the children and provides an essentially compensatory environment.

Playwork in practice

Playworkers see children as "the subjects of their own development," and play as a process of both "being and becoming" (Sturrock 2007). In other words, play has both immediate and longer-term benefits. It is only during play that children are likely to experience being in control of their own destiny. As has already been said, in practice playwork is substantially about creating environments that enable children to play freely. The most effective playwork environment, therefore, has little intervention from the playworker once the basic parameters have been set. Put simply, the role of the playworker is to provide the setting, the tools, and the materials, and leave the rest to the children, albeit having regard for their safety and security. In the words of John Portchmouth (1969, p. 7): "It helps if someone no matter how lightly puts in our way the means of making use of what we find." Portchmouth speaks of being taken to the beach, given a bucket and spade, and left to play in whatever way he wanted. He didn't need an instruction booklet, or a program designed by an adult. The basic tools, and a flexible environment, were enough for him to engage creatively with the play process.

Identifying and removing barriers to play

Unfortunately, as has already been discussed, many modern environments contain elements that act against the play process. Therefore, the initial task of the playworker is usually to analyze the environment in order to identify and remove any barriers to the children's play. This could mean something complex like negotiating the closure of a busy street to remove a traffic danger; or something simple like picking up broken bottles that have somehow found their way onto the outdoor space of an after-school club. Sometimes the playworker will be acting as an advocate for children whose voice is not being heard. In some cases the barriers are not obvious, and the playworker will need to get to know the local culture before being able to judge what the real obstacles are. In many modern communities the biggest obstacle to free play is the careless disregard of children's rights by adults, and in particular Article 31 of the UN Convention on the Rights of the Child, which recognizes the child's right to play (UNICEF 1991).

Enriching the play environment

Having identified, and hopefully removed, the barriers to play, the playworker's next task is to enrich the child's play environment in order to stimulate the play process. This has sometimes been interpreted as a form of "scaffolding," for example by Staempfli (2009, p.271), who suggests that "play scaffolding enables children to take control of their own experiences. The role of the playworker is that of unobtrusive guide," a professional who "reinvigorates the process of child development through play" (Brown 2003c, p.51).

The concept of scaffolding was originally developed by Bruner et al. (2010) to describe the way in which an adult might provide a carefully designed structure to enable children to learn. That level of adult-led intervention would not be accepted in the playwork approach. Although intervention is sometimes necessary, in all cases the child's agenda has to be taken as the starting point for playwork interventions. Enriching the play environment is not about promoting an adult agenda of specific learning outcomes, but rather adopting an holistic approach to development, and accepting that children are "competent to meet their play needs" so long as they are given appropriate opportunities (Melville 1999, p.71). A number of factors have to be taken into account when considering how best to create a play-friendly environment. These have been summarized as: freedom; flexibility; socialization and social interaction; physical activity; intellectual stimulation; creativity and problem-solving; emotional equilibrium; self-discovery; ethical stance; adult/child relationships; and the general appeal of elements such as humor, color, etc. (Brown 2003c, p.64). There is a striking synergy between these elements and the detrimental factors summarized in previous chapters.

For many playworkers the most significant theory underpinning their work is *compound flexibility*, i.e. "the interrelationship between a flexible/adaptable environment and the gradual development of flexibility/adaptability in the child" (Brown 2003c, p.53). According to Sutton-Smith the function of play is "adaptive variability" (1997, p.231). Taking these two concepts together we can infer that the role of the playworker is to create flexible environments which are substantially adaptable or controllable by the children. One way of doing this is to ensure there are lots of "loose parts" in the play environment. When explaining his "theory of loose parts," Nicholson suggested "in any environment both the degree of inventiveness and creativity, and the possibility of discovery, are directly proportional to the number and kind of variables in it" (1971, p.30). Thus, a room full of cardboard boxes, packing crates, old clothes, etc. is more likely to stimulate creative play than a fixed climbing frame.

Example of research:

Broadhead et al. (2011) conducted a study of a loose parts project at the Eureka! Children's Museum in Halifax. A room was set aside in the museum and stocked with a wide range of open-ended play materials, such as boxes, tyres, rope, paper, tubes, etc. Eureka! enablers agreed to undertake observations using a specifically designed observation schedule which provided mainly quantitative data with some qualitative comments from parents/carers. The research team undertook non-partic- ipant, narrative observations, discussions with parents/carers and conversations with enablers which provided complementary qualitative data.

The team gathered a mass of observational data, which they then attempted to interpret, albeit recognizing the pitfalls of such an approach, i.e. adults often completely misinterpret what children's play actually means for the child. Nevertheless, here are three examples, with the team suggesting some interesting interpretations. A girl wrote: "keep out of my den," which suggests that personal space is important and the creation of it is empowering. The most common activity was climbing into a box and sitting there quietly, which has something to do with personal space, privacy, and emotional equilibrium (one child climbed in a box and went to sleep). Two boys worked together to make a den and then coloured the outside of the den. The team didn't know if these boys were familiar with one another but suggest collaborative activity takes many skills of negotiation and information exchange. Cooperation is an intellectually challenging activity.

Broadhead et al. (2011) say they cannot draw any strong conclusions about the integration of this approach into the rest of the museum because this was not part of their evaluation, but they are very clear about the substantial benefits to be gained from developing the initiative. They state the loose parts environment encourages: creativity and imagination, social interaction and cooperative activity. It offers environmental interaction, cognitive stimulation, new discovery, opportu- nities for combinatorial activity, for privacy and the creation of personal space.

Reflections on the research

Although it is arguable that a children's museum is not a true playwork setting, the lessons from this study are nevertheless pertinent. There are many positive outcomes from the loose parts approach for both the individual child, and also the setting as a whole. Working with children when they are in creative mode is a joy for the staff, which is clearly a desirable outcome. Furthermore, the loose parts approach is inexpensive. Most playwork settings work to a tight budget, so from the management point of view, the cost savings of this approach should be attractive. Finally, in a small way, the loose parts approach is beneficial for society as a whole. At its heart is the concept of recycling waste materials, which is clearly good for the environment.

> ### Activity 3
>
> Taylor (2008) has explored the synergies between playwork and the theory of loose parts in some detail. She suggests the theory was especially suited to the 1970s, where it "touched contemporaneous preoccupations with egalitarianism, self-governance and tempering the impacts of urbanization, with creativity and alternatives to the established order" (2008, p. 43).
>
> The concept of heuristic play was first developed in the 1980s (Goldschmied & Jackson 1994). It involves children in the exploration of the properties of materials and artifacts; in particular the sort of materials to be found in the average household—pots, pans, wool, strips of material, etc. The approach has considerable overlaps with the theory of loose parts. Study the concept of heuristic play in greater depth (Riddall-Leech 2009) and consider its synergies with the loose parts approach. Where do the two approaches converge/diverge? Reflecting on the previous research example, do you think these two concepts are still relevant today?

> ### Key points:
>
> - Good playwork practice involves identifying and removing barriers to play before the full benefits of the play process can be felt.
> - The role of the playworker is to create flexible environments which are substantially adaptable or controllable by the children.
> - Playworkers use a range of techniques aimed at enhancing the children's play environment.
> - One such approach is based on Nicholson's (1971) theory of loose parts, another on the concept of heuristic play (Goldschmied & Jackson 1994).

Interview with Susan Waltham about her research

Susan Waltham, Senior Lecturer, Leeds Metropolitan University

Fraser Brown: How do you see the research in relation to your work in a more formal setting?

Susan Waltham: The loose parts project at Eureka! has informed my teaching of undergraduate students, particularly those on initial teacher education courses. It will also impact on my teaching at Masters level on the MA childhood studies and the MA early years.

The findings have strengthened my stance on the use of open-ended resources with learners, and the use of the emergent curriculum. The activity was child-led and facilitated by the adults present (the museum enablers and parents/carers). My image of the child as a natural researcher and scientist has also been supported by this research.

Fraser Brown: **What did you discover about the process of observing children's play from doing this research?**
Susan Waltham: The tension between participant and non-participant observation was clear in this study. Children approached and included the adults who were observing them, asking for support in using the resources and finding appropriate equipment such as glue, sticky tape, scissors etc. The role of the enabler at the museum was obviously clear to the children; the children expected the enablers to facilitate and scaffold their work.

The introduction of observation as a research tool to the enablers at Eureka! was an interesting exercise. Many of the enablers were not familiar with observing children for research purposes, and how observation would address the aims of the study. A pro forma observation sheet was provided so that enablers could comment on criteria that were predetermined for the purposes of this study.

Fraser Brown: **Did anything surprise you about either what you observed, or the way the research developed?**
Susan Waltham: I was surprised about the amount of collaboration between children who were actually strangers to each other. This is particularly relevant to this context as, unless the children are there as a school party, children are accessing the galleries in the museum with their parents/carers and siblings.

I was so pleased to note that the children adopted a very independent stance from their parents and their teachers. This indicated that the children did feel secure in this context and were happy to be in control of their immediate environment and activities.

The research allayed a number of fears about the use of loose parts within the context of Eureka! The National Children's Museum. Parents showed very positive responses to the provision, the children demonstrated levels of involvement and concentration that were quite striking for this age group, and the transportation of the loose parts to other galleries did not occur.

The wider benefits of playwork

Improving confidence and competence

Playwork seeks to encourage the growth of confidence and self-esteem. This is achieved in part by providing an environment that is both physically safe and personally secure, but nevertheless offers children the opportunity to take risks and experience challenges. In that regard we are not speaking only of physical experiences, but also social and emotional ones. For example, every time a child jumps out from behind a tree and shouts "boo" at another child, s/he is taking a risk. At best the result may be an extension of friendly play. At worst the action may result in rejection, or even violence (Gladwin 2005). A good quality playwork experience will offer children the opportunity to initiate risky behavior, sometimes within a secure context, but not always. Indeed Hughes (1996, p. 19) says:

> Because of its powerful role in the development of survival skills, a comprehensive play experience must contain a measure of actual risk-taking behavior, i.e. behavior where at least the possibility of pain and/or injury is real.

However, it is important for playworkers to understand that every child has her/his own limits. One child's slightly risky challenge could possibly be another child's dangerous situation. Therefore, it is not the playworker's role deliberately to introduce risky situations. That would be dangerous for some children. Rather they should be prepared to stand back when they witness children taking risks. The problem for the playworker is where and when to intervene. Obviously no one wants children to hurt themselves, but when children are playing accidents will happen. There is an adventure playground in Bradford where all parents are advised as a matter of course that their children are likely to have accidents while playing in that setting.

That is an approach which has the support of the UK's Health & Safety Executive. In their document titled *Playgrounds—risks, benefits and choices* (Ball 2002) we find the following statement:

> … the crucial societal problem of playgrounds and their provision relates less to safety of playgrounds *per se*, than to the issue of how to realise for children the full range of social, physical, emotional and cognitive benefits associated with play (one of which is considered to be the learning experience gained from exposure to modest risk). Second to this is the issue of how to balance these

positive attributes against the inevitable risk of injury which any activity, including play, generates.

Unfortunately, in complete contrast to the HSE's approach, for many years in both the USA and the UK the more restrictive arm of the safety lobby held sway, with the result that children's playgrounds tend to be less adventurous today. There is some evidence that this is a worldwide phenomenon, stretching across all five continents (Lester & Russell 2010). However, there are signs of a change. In the UK this overprotective lobby may well have had its day. In a recent *Position Statement* the UK Play Safety Forum said: "Risk-taking is an essential feature of play provision, and of all environments in which children legitimately spend time at play" (Play Safety Forum 2008, p. 2).

Developing unique relationships

One of the most significant elements of the playwork approach is the way in which relationships are made with the children. If the child/adult relationship is effective, there is a good chance of not only helping children with their problems, but also raising their self-esteem generally. Most adults who come into contact with children bring their own agenda to that relationship. For example, teachers have an obligation to teach an agreed curriculum (a set of adult priorities). Doctors, social workers, even parents, invariably have their own adult priorities. The playworker is unusual in as much as s/he attempts to suspend personal prejudice, and go along with the flow of the children's needs and tastes.

This brings us to the concept of "negative capability." The poet John Keats (1817) suggested this was a characteristic of all creative minds. He recommended the complete suspension of all prejudices and preconceptions as a prelude to opening up the creative flow of the mind. The similarity between this approach to creativity and one of the most fundamental aspects of the child-adult relationship in playwork has been explored by Fisher (2008), who suggests that playworkers have to guard against entering the play environment with their own preconceptions and prejudices. Only then will they truly be there for the child. This approach requires a great sensitivity to the learning potential of the playwork setting, and means the playworker has to be prepared to stand back when others might be inclined to rush in.

Example of research:

Maureen Palmer (2008) draws on her experience of working on Cornwallis Adventure Playground in the London Borough of Islington during the 1980s. She makes extensive use of conversations that took place during the production of *Reflections on Adventure Play* (Palmer 2002), a DVD presenting some of the data from a longitudinal study of children, young people and their families on the adventure playground. She draws on video recordings, oral tapes, daybooks and numerous discussions. At the heart of the research is a series of powerful reflections by adults who used the playground as children. They were especially asked to focus on what the playground meant to them. Palmer focuses on the key themes that emerge from those conversations:

- A sense of belonging or feeling part of something.
- The idea of community and personal identity, one developing in conjunction with the other.
- The sense that they were free to try and do anything, nothing being out of bounds.
- Their sense of control over the space, how it changed and developed.
- The sense that they could be the catalyst for change.
- Their sense that they were solidly held, respected, valued and cared for.
- Their confidence that they had aware, thoughtful and committed playworkers, who would go the extra mile for them.

Palmer concludes that the adventure playground acted as the hub of the community, and that this was possible because of the nature of the playwork practised there, and the way it worked with the natural rhythms of the community within which it operated. She speaks of an "important organic process that is increasingly missing from children's play spaces," and she contends that "an adventure playground is a children's space, where children can change and grow in their own way, and by osmosis develop a community culture of which they are the key and the catalyst" (Palmer 2008, pp.132–3).

In a further piece of research in 2006, Palmer tested out some of the key learning points that had emerged from this earlier study. She negotiated with the playworkers of another adventure playground to open two nights a week over the summer until 9.00 p.m. The research involved observations and interviews with children and parents on site, and Palmer maintained detailed reflective diaries. Palmer concluded that this later opening showed a marked change in the way the parents and the children saw their playground and their playworkers. The playground began to feel more a part of the community. Indeed the community responded in a number of positive ways. For example, several different mums came to cook for the whole playground in the evening. Parents spoke about how the late opening allowed them to get all their tasks done, and still get their children to the playground for several hours to play. It also gave them the opportunity to meet other parents and children. Palmer (p. 135) includes a number of delightful and revealing quotes from the children regarding the late opening:

"It's somewhere to get away from TV and family"—9-year-old

"We wouldn't be allowed to play out this late if the playground closed earlier"—10-year-old

"During term time it would be good to close at 7.00pm"—12-year-old

"I like the late nights when it's quieter, and you can go on the swings and I like to play with my friends and we sit up there [she points to a platform on one of the structures] and watch the sunset. It goes down over there, and we watch it till it disappears"—8-year-old

Palmer (pp.135–6) reaches a number of strong conclusions, which she describes as "the implications for playwork of re-tuning to community rhythms":

- In order to provide safe spaces in hostile environments, or for children who have a bad time at school and need a place to be loved and valued in their day, opening times should fit with the patterns of community life.
- Playgrounds should operate across the age ranges—there should be no false segregation of ages, based merely on what goes on in schools.
- Playworkers need to be planned and focussed upon giving away power to enable the children's own culture to grow, for them to feel their own sense of self, and feel they are powerful people in our communities.
- Playworkers must establish an environment that says anything is possible, and an approach that shouts loudly "give it a go and see, explore it, test it, and it's okay to do it here."
- Consistency and continuity are essential—there must be real long-term commitment and playworkers must always being willing to go the extra mile.
- Children must be enabled to take control, take real risks, and break the chains of learned helplessness.
- Playworkers must be aware and forward-thinking, and able to respond in the time and way the child needs.
- Finally, and most important—our children need to feel loved.

Activity 4

This is a powerful piece of research, which challenges us to rethink our attitudes not only to the broad issue of children's place in society, but also to some very specific issues such as opening times. Consider the socio-cultural obstacles to Palmer's recommendations for retuning to community rhythms. For example, what would be the obstacles to opening until later in the evening? What would be the arguments for and against opening a play project to children of all ages?

> **Key points:**
>
> - Playwork seeks to encourage the growth of confidence and self-esteem.
> - Risk and challenge are an essential part of children's play.
> - We have over-sanitized play provision. Accidents will happen while children are playing.
> - Playworkers are the only adults who work with children who don't take control of the child's agenda.
> - The mindset of "negative capability" allows playworkers to enter the child's environment in a non-directive, non-judgmental, and non-prejudicial way.
> - The strong child/adult relationships formed in playwork settings are at the heart of any successful project.
> - An adventure playground is at its best when it is truly at the heart of its local community, and reflects the very nature of that community.

Analyzing the impact of playwork

As we have seen, at its most effective a single playwork project is capable of changing the lives of many hundreds, perhaps thousands of children. It is also capable of having a widespread positive impact on whole communities. Why is the playwork relationship so powerful?

At the level of the individual child, one of the reasons is that when children are playing they are "learning to control their own little microcosm of the world" (Sutton-Smith 1992). In other words, they are in charge of things. In most cases when adults come into the child's world they take control. That creates an adult/child relationship which is rooted in power. In most cases (although not always) the adult will be exercising that power in the best interests of the child. Nevertheless, children see themselves as the subordinate player in the relationship. In contrast, the playworker does not take control, but merely provides a safe and secure environment within which the child may play freely. Consequently, children very quickly come to regard playworkers in a different light to other adults in their lives. It is hard to define that relationship. There are elements of friendship and even equality, and yet the child still sees the playworker as an adult. In times of personal trouble, the child will very often approach the playworker first, before any other adult—especially when an adult is the cause of the problem. Playworkers need to be aware of this likelihood, and trained in how to cope in the best interests of the child.

At the level of the wider community, playwork settings often become a focus for community activity. According to Chilton (2003, p.127), "an effective playworker requires knowledge of ... the local community: its characteristics and personalities." A playworker of long standing may even become one of those personalities (see the example of The Venture, mentioned previously in this chapter). This is not hard to achieve, so long as parents see that the playworkers are genuinely there for their children. If that is the case then parents will begin to trust the playworker in the same way as their children. In an ideal world a playwork setting can become a place where the whole community plays together. However, it should never be forgotten that this is the children's facility, and their parents are only there by invitation.

Example of research:

Between 2001 and 2005 Barnardo's and the Children's Play Council worked together to manage Better Play—a £10.8 million grant program funded by the New Opportunities Fund with money from the national lottery. The Better Play program offered grants throughout England to community organizations or organizations acting on behalf of communities, to improve play opportunities for children aged 5–16 years. The program funded 225 projects in three distinct phases:

1 Organizations interested in delivering play services and developing local play policies and strategies.
2 Play projects that promoted good practice—as defined in *Best Play* (NPFA 2000).
3 Projects that promoted inclusive play.

The third focus was a direct result of the fact that very few inclusive projects were funded in the first two phases. Consequently, the funding in the final phase was aimed at both mainstream services becoming inclusive of disabled children and specialist services working towards becoming inclusive of all children. In the words of Ludvigsen et al. (2005, p.4), "the primary aim of the programme was that by the end of the funded year more disabled and non-disabled children would be sharing play provision and playing together."

An evaluation of the program was undertaken by Youlden & Harrison (2006) using the seven Best Play objectives and four of the Better Play program objectives as their broad evaluative criteria. Six projects were studied in depth. They used a wide range of techniques, including introductory letters, interviews, discussion groups, observations, worker diaries, graffiti walls, questionnaires, telephone interviews, and activity books. This last method was intended to ensure the involvement of participants with low levels of literacy. Their data was then subjected to thematic content analysis, and finally they were able to reach a number of very positive conclusions about the benefits of playwork projects:

- Children are introduced to a wide range of experiences that they would otherwise not have.
- The new experiences challenge the children physically, creatively, and socially.
- Those experiences are thoroughly enjoyed and the children want to repeat them.
- Children are provided with a real alternative to playing on the streets.
- There are increased levels of social contact, with both peers and adults.
- Disabled and non-disabled children all benefit from that sort of interaction.
- Children's social skills and self-esteem are enhanced.
- There are benefits for children's physical, social, and emotional well-being.
- Children gain a deeper understanding of their own and other people's cultures.
- Improve children's knowledge of the natural environment.
- Provide a space where parents feel confident about their children's safety.
- Make a contribution to social cohesion and friendship networks within the community.
- Offer employment and voluntary work.

Youlden and Harrison found that all six projects achieved all of the Best Play objectives, albeit they voiced concerns about whether it was possible to generalize on the basis of such a small sample. Nevertheless they state:

> The presence of skilled and experienced playworkers enhanced the range of choices children had and children were able to exert control … All six projects allowed and encouraged children to challenge themselves and test their own boundaries … The relationships between staff and children were important … the way in which staff supported children had an impact on aspects of the children's self-esteem." (2006, p. 6)

Thus, their overall conclusion was that these play projects had wide ranging identifiable benefits for the children and their communities.

Activity 5

This section has made the argument that playworkers have a unique relationship with children—a relationship that cannot be matched by any other adult who comes into contact with children. Do you think people such as teachers, nursery workers, and children's nurses would be prepared to accept that? If not, what sort of arguments do you think they could make in support of their case? Consider this in light of your own experience of those professions.

Key points:

- Good quality playwork provision has the potential to have a positive impact on the lives of individual children, and also the wider community.

- Individual children will quickly form trusting relationships with playworkers.
- The wider community will come to trust the playworkers because of their work with the children.
- Playwork introduces children to a wide range of experiences.
- Playwork increases the levels of social contact with both peers and adults, and enhances the child's self-esteem.
- Playwork raises the profile of children within the wider community.
- Playwork produces benefits for children's physical, social, and emotional well-being.
- Playwork has the potential to bring benefit to all children regardless of ability, gender, ethnicity, etc.

Summary

This chapter has highlighted the following points:

- Playwork is a well-established profession in the UK, with its own unique set of values.
- Playworkers focus on the freely chosen, personally directed, and intrinsically motivated aspects of play.
- In practice playwork generally involves identifying and removing the barriers to play, and then enhancing the children's play environment.
- Playwork improves the confidence and competence of children, not least by allowing them to engage with risk and challenge.
- A unique sort of child/adult relationship lies at the heart of the playwork approach.
- Playworkers help to enhance children's self-esteem by treating children with respect, and placing their agenda at the heart of all decisions.
- Playwork has wide-ranging benefits for both individual children and the wider community.

Further reading

Davy, A. & Gallagher, J. (2006) *New Playwork: Play and care for children 4–16*. 4th edition. London: Thomson Learning. This textbook covers the key areas of practical playwork. Topics covered include child development, playwork principles and the role of the playworker, policy and legislation, creating play spaces, relationships with children and parents, behavior, inclusion, reflective practice, teamwork, child protection, health and safety, and playwork and the wider community

Hughes, B. (2001) *Evolutionary Playwork and Reflective Analytic Practice*. London: Routledge. Explores the complexities of children's play, and examines its meaning and purpose. Considers the fundamentals of evolutionary playwork, and looks at some key theoretical concepts underlying playwork.

Sturrock, G. & Else, P. (1998) The playground as therapeutic space: playwork as healing, in *Proceedings of the IPA/USA Triennial National Conference, Play in a Changing Society: Research, Design, Application*. June 1998, Colorado. USA Presents an argument that as natural play space is gradually being eroded to the detriment of children, the role of the playworker is changing to encompass a more therapeutic function.

Rethinking play 7

Chapter Outline

Introduction and key questions

This chapter has a rather different format to the preceding chapters. In this chapter we will focus on our conclusions from the preceding text. The chapter is structured around a number of themes that imply the need for rethinking. In this way we will be addressing a number of key questions:

- How can we change the public's general negativity towards children playing?
- How can we best promote the child's right to play?
- What is the significance of play in developing survival skills?

- Is it acceptable to expect children to pay for their play?
- How can we make going to school a more playful (enjoyable) experience?
- How can we reduce the stress in our children's lives?
- How can we expand the playwork profession?

The public's view of children

In October 2011 the research organization ICM released the results of a poll commissioned by the children's charity Barnardo's which revealed that British adults have a very negative view of children. The poll showed nearly half the UK population (49 per cent) agree that children today are beginning to behave like animals. The findings also show 44 per cent agree that children in the UK are becoming feral. Nearly half (47 per cent) agree that the trouble with young people is they are angry, violent, and abusive. One in four (25 per cent) think children who behave badly or antisocially are beyond help by the age of ten.

It is quite disappointing that the British public holds this negative view of children, despite the majority being well-behaved, attending school (NAO 2005), taking part in activities, and a significant number contributing to their communities and volunteering (Atkinson 2010). For example, the organization C4EO (2011) found "around threequarters of all young people participate in some form of positive activities." Barnardo's chief executive Anne Marie Carrie responded boldly to this depressing outcome, saying:

> We seem to have forgotten the fact that most children are well-behaved and instead we are unquestioningly accepting a stereotype of young people as criminal and revolting. But it's never too late to believe in children and change their life story.

However, there may be something of a vicious circle in the UK:

> Majority culture in the UK does not generally value children and children's points of view very highly. The belief that "children should be seen and not heard" may have its origins in Victorian times but it is far from dead and buried today. (Wertheimer 1997, p.10)

Parents may possibly like their own children, but that is not the same thing as liking children generally.

The play environment is the whole environment

Unfortunately, children's play is a serious casualty of this negative inflexible attitude towards children. The most natural forms of playful behavior are inevitably noisy, messy, and physically boisterous. Consequently, when children are playing naturally in the outdoors they are likely to be seen as trouble-makers, indulging in anti-social behavior, when all they are actually doing is having fun. Colin Ward's observation from more than thirty years ago confronts us with a dilemma:

> One thing that the observation of children makes clear, though it has only recently entered the world of reports and textbooks, and has yet to affect environmental policies, is that children *will* play everywhere and with anything (1978, p. 86).

This is a theme taken up by Hughes more recently when he said play is a sphere of activity that involves the child in "an interdependent relationship with everything else around them" (1996a, p. 22).

If we accept the Hughes/Ward proposition that it is only natural for children to play everywhere and with everything, then we have to find a way of changing the public perception of children as being a nuisance. Otherwise, children will constantly come into conflict with adults unnecessarily. Should we be looking for a compromise that will achieve some sort of balance, or would that actually be betraying our children's birthright, as enshrined in Article 31 of the United Nations Convention on the Rights of the Child (UNICEF 1991)? Perhaps it is time for the signatories to rethink, and instead of paying lip service to Article 31 of the UNCRC, begin to enact further legislation to ensure that the right to play is properly accepted. For example, it would be simple enough to identify playspace as exactly that, and guarantee its designation in perpetuity. In connection with this it would be crucial to recognize that playspace includes all spaces where children play—not just parks and playgrounds, but also natural areas. In addition an imaginative government might start taking unused private land into public ownership and designating it as playspace, where it was suitable. Of course the USA has to take another step over and above that, and sign up to the UNCRC. America is currently the only country in the United Nations not to have done so. In contrast the African member states of the Organisation of African Unity, in adopting Article 12 of the African Charter for the Rights and Welfare of the Child (ACRWC 1990), adopted Article 31 of the UNCRC in its entirety.

Article 31 and the Charter for Children's Play

Secondly, it is important for those responsible for all forms of play provision to understand that the UNCRC is supposed to be read as a whole. Individual articles are not supposed to be taken in isolation. Given that the benefits of play are so widespread, it follows that the right to play is affected by several articles of the UNCRC. For example, the following articles all affect children's play provision: non-discrimination; the best interests of the child; the right to express a view and to be listened to; freedom of expression; freedom of association and the right to protection from abuse and neglect. Additional articles supporting the rights of specific groups of children—for example, disabled children, children from minority ethnic groups, refugees and asylum-seekers, and those in public care—must also be respected (Cole-Hamilton 2008).

Partly as a response to the need for a generic approach to the child's right to play, the national support organization Play England developed the Charter for Children's Play (2007). This sets out a vision for play, plus basic principles of what play means for children. The eight key statements are:

- Children have the right to play.
- Every child needs time and space to play.
- Adults should let children play.
- Children should be able to play freely in their local areas.
- Children value and benefit from staffed play provision.
- Children's play is enriched by skilled playworkers.
- Children need time and space to play at school.
- Children sometimes need extra support to enjoy their right to play.

In order to become a member of Play England you have to sign up to the Charter. It would be a giant step in the right direction if public authorities could be persuaded to sign up to the Charter.

At the inaugural meeting of the National Playing Fields Association in 1926, the Chairman read the following statement from former British Prime Minister, David Lloyd George:

> The right to play is the child's first claim on the community. Play is nature's training for life. No community can infringe that right without doing enduring harm to the minds and bodies of its citizens.

If the present public attitude to children playing is allowed to continue there can be no doubt that we risk doing enduring harm to the minds and bodies of our citizens.

Re-educating the public

At the same time as taking measures to change the public perception about the importance of play, it would be necessary to clarify what it is we are talking about. Exactly what is so special about children's play? Why is it worth making all this fuss about? There would be no point in designating children's playspace without making it clear what sort of activities will take place there. If we fail to do that, then the public will interpret the normal rough and tumble of children's play as violent, aggressive behavior; they will view all that slightly chaotic creative activity as anarchistic and messy; they will think teasing is actually bullying; they will see risk-taking as reckless and dangerous behavior. We need to educate the general public about the reality of play—or maybe we just need to remind them of what it was like to be a child at play.

For many years play has generally been associated in the literature with some sort of positive affect (Singer & Singer 2005; Garvey 1990; Krasnor & Pepler 1980). Freud (1920) suggested it was substantially about children reframing their world to make it less frightening. However, that is not always the case; sometimes play itself is scary, and it is often deeply competitive (Sutton-Smith 1997). Of course the truth is that even when play is brutal and destructive, it is still valuable in developmental terms, helping to teach children about hierarchy, status, boundaries, etc.—but perhaps it is unrealistic to expect people who think children are feral animals to move so far in their thinking that they come to regard the darker sides of play as acceptable. Instead Brown (2009) suggests we need to concentrate on its value for us as a species.

Developing survival skills

There is a tendency in Western societies to view children as adults in waiting, and play as a preparation mechanism for adulthood. Play is often depicted as a practice ground for adult roles (see Bjorklund 2007 for a full discussion of this issue). An example of that way of thinking would be the idea that children play "mothers and fathers" in preparation for parenting roles later in life. However, Sutton-Smith (1997) says that sort of idyllic view of play is a trivialization of something that has significance for the development of the whole human species. In fact he suggests it is the multi-faceted nature of play that equips children with the full range of survival skills that enable them to cope with the world around them, as they develop into adults. Sutton-Smith describes play as a "facsimilization of the struggle for survival" (p. 231).

In a later work Sutton-Smith (2008) lays out in detail the way in which, through a dialectical process of action and rebuttal, we learn the survival skills that enable us to cope with the daily trials of life. For example, playful teasing involves a sort of mild harassment which when met with resilience may be seen to prepare us for social initiation procedures in later life; risk-taking involves danger being confronted with courage, which prepares us for the chances we take with our physical and economic fate; the competitive anger experienced during contests and organized games mimics the real world of combat, wars, and predation.

Sutton-Smith (1997) also suggests that play should be seen as an evolutionary mechanism; the means by which human beings adapt to an ever-changing world. He says we are born with the potential to be adaptable, but it is only during play that we develop and refine that ability. We know that play activity stimulates the brain by activating a "fertilizer" known as brain-derived neurotrophic factor (BDNF). This not only helps to enhance the development of the higher brain, but also enables better management of emotions and stress (Sunderland 2006). Play also stimulates the release of opioids, which in turn appear to cause brain cells to retain their "plasticity". Sutton-Smith (1997) and many who have followed (e.g. Hughes 2001; Brown 2009) suggest that if we don't play, our brain cells rigidify, and our flexibility of thought is reduced. Ultimately we become unable to cope with change, which could have dire consequences both for the individual and for the future of our species (Sutton-Smith 2008).

Thus, Sutton-Smith is making the not inconsiderable claim that play is at the very heart of the evolutionary process. Perhaps if public authorities come to realize this, they will take children's play more seriously. Perhaps if individual members of the public can accept this, then they may begin to see children as human beings, rather than animals.

The importance of free unstructured play, especially play fighting

A recent report into the effects of television on the healthy development of young children by the American Academy of Pediatrics (2011 p.2) stated:

> Unstructured play time is more valuable for the developing brain than electronic media. Children learn to think creatively, problem-solve, and develop reasoning and motor skills at early ages through unstructured, unplugged play.

We know very well that play has clear social, physical, cognitive and emotional benefits (Milteer & Ginsburg 2012). We know also that play has therapeutic benefits (Brown & Webb 2005), but the benefits of intentional paradox and deliberate uncertainty are less well recognized. These two extracts from Lester & Russell's IPA paper (2010) express this very well:

> … play is about creating a world in which, for that moment, children are in control and can seek out uncertainty in order to triumph over it. (p. x)

> In play, order (as a representation of dominant adult organisation) is opposed, inverted and subverted. Spinka et al. (2001) suggest that play's evolutionary origins may be found in the deliberate creation of uncertainty and unbalance in order to regain control, as training for the unexpected. Expressed simply, children at play are in control of being out of control (Gordon & Esbjorn-Hargens 2007). (Lester & Russell 2010, p. 8)

For Sutton-Smith (1997, p. 231) the value of this apparently illogical paradoxical behavior is "to reinforce the organism's variability in the face of rigidifications of successful adaptation." In other words, whenever human beings conquer a new challenge they are inclined to set in stone the behavior that achieved that success. The function of play is constantly to present alternatives, and so stop us becoming rigid in our behavior patterns.

The leading neuroscientist Jaak Panksepp (1998) says there are eight genetically ingrained emotional systems in the brain: rage, fear, separation, distress, seeking, care, play, and lust (which develops during puberty). He says that during periods when children are engaged in seeking, caring, or playing there is a release of opioids into the frontal lobes of the brain. Put simply, this is good for us. It makes us feel happy, calm, and satisfied. According to Panksepp (2008) and Pellis & Pellis (2009) rough and tumble play (play fighting) is the most valuable form of play activity, because during rough and tumble play children experience all three of the positive emotions. This hypothesis has been tested out on rats. Apparently rats start to engage in rough and tumble play around the age of 6 months. If they are not allowed to engage in that sort of play during this crucial period, they grow up severely deficient in social skills. There is a growing body of thought that is linking the prevalence of ADHD in modern societies to the reduction in physically active play behavior.

Panksepp (2008) is so concerned about our present negative attitude towards children's play that he suggests we should consider Plato's concept of play sanctuaries for children. Plato thought that great benefit accrued from engagement in free play, and proposed the creation of sanctuaries where children were free to engage in such activity. Plato felt that if children lacked the opportunity to play, they could never become fully human. The following extract summarizes Panksepp's view:

> So where might Plato's play sanctuaries fit in our world, where nature has been removed from the lives of most of our children and most kids are over-protected, regimented, and TV-vegetated; where most young children have too few rough and tumble play partners (organized sports and video games being a pale imitation for real PLAY); where most parents and educators don't even recognize the profound value of real play for their children; where many believe that treating children like little adults helps rear social brains? ... It is reasonable to postulate that full maturation of higher brain social networks (perhaps even "mirror neurons") requires full immersion in real PLAY. If families can no longer provide such childhood luxuries, then perhaps it should become a societal responsibility to create "play sanctuaries"—places where we combine the best of play and the best of emotionally fulfilling education. (Panksepp 2008, p.76)

This argument has clear implications for the playwork profession, either in as much as most playwork settings could be regarded as "play sanctuaries," or in the suggestion that all schools should employ playwork staff.

Play warehouses—the commodification of play

Another way in which it might be thought these play sanctuaries could be created is through the proliferation of play warehouses that have sprung up in recent years (McKendrick 1996b). However, that sort of commodification of play is anathema to most play theorists, and also to playworkers who espouse the "three frees" approach in their work. For most observers it is doubtful whether pay to play warehouses really address the play needs of most children. They clearly provide an exciting physical space, and offer opportunities for one very specific form of social interaction (i.e. engaging in social contact with children you have not met before), but beyond that it is doubtful whether they offer much long-term benefit. Furthermore, McKendrick (1999b) expresses a concern that they might come to be regarded as a replacement for collective public play spaces. This is a troubling thought, and one that must be resisted. In truth the idea that children should have to pay to play goes against the grain for anyone who accepts that the freedom to play is a child's right.

School should be a playful experience

Another setting where we might consider placing Plato's play sanctuaries is the school—after all, that is where children already spend a great deal of their time. Unfortunately, school is too often a deeply unpopular place among the very children that it is supposed to serve (Willingham 2009). Many schools have interpreted the Every Child Matters agenda (in the UK) and the No Child Left Behind agenda (in the USA) as being a call for more classroom time (see Chapter 2). Sadly, in that regard they are reflecting what most politicians seem to think—namely that getting our schools' teaching methods right is the single best thing we can do for our children.

On the contrary, as we have seen in Chapter 2 of this book, there are numerous studies that suggest it would be far more effective simply to empower children to play. Sutton-Smith says that after moments of playing everyone feels better and subsequent events work better.

> The opposite of play—if redefined in terms which stress its reinforcing optimism and excitement—is not work, it is depression. Players come out of their ludic paradoxes ... with renewed belief in the worthwhileness of merely living. (Sutton-Smith 1999, p. 254)

The logic of this as applied to the school day would be for the curriculum to be designed around children's play opportunities—not in the current half-hearted sense, where play is sometimes used as a tool to enable teachers to trick children into learning the things that adults think are important. Instead, if there were as much time given to play in the school day as was given over to adult-directed teaching, there would be a double benefit. Not only would the children have the opportunity genuinely to learn while they are playing, but also when they returned to the classroom, they would be so much more ready to learn because of the energizing nature of free play. What we are proposing here is a school day that is extended to accommodate working parents, but structured around alternate 45-minute periods of free play and classroom learning. It would not be reasonable to expect the teachers to fulfill the dual role implicit in this arrangement, and so this revised approach would involve the employment of playworkers alongside teachers.

There are two more steps our schools can take to make themselves more helpful in addressing all the needs of the children they serve. Firstly, they should be telling the children about the importance of informal play, and encouraging them to engage in free play, rather than concentrating on homework. Secondly, they should be opening their playgrounds after school. Most school playgrounds are a wasted resource, as they are often the only large open space within a community, and yet the gates are often locked by 6.00pm and all over the weekend. Employing playworkers to work during the school day and at weekends would be a novel and imaginative step towards making the school into the hub of its community.

Stress—positive, tolerable, and toxic

Another way in which teachers could be more helpful to the children with whom they work would be to alter their approach to intervention. The National Scientific Council on the Developing Child (2005) has identified three forms of stress: positive, tolerable, and toxic.

Positive stress is essentially beneficial. This is where the child may be up against a deadline, or taking part in a competition, or simply engaged in play fighting. In all such cases there will be a brief exhilarating release of adrenalin, lots of excitement, and in general a positive outcome. For most children the process is more important than the product when they are playing, and so they will not be greatly disturbed by losing a competition.

Tolerable stress occurs where the child experiences acute moments of anxiety or distress, but the event takes place within a supportive atmosphere. An obvious example would be a death in a child's family, and the subsequent grieving process. The child is likely to be deeply disturbed and upset in the short term, but in the long run manages the stress effectively as a result of the strong emotional support of family and friends.

Toxic stress occurs where a child has no control over her/his own destiny. The irony of our school system is that teachers are far more likely to intervene in the case of positive stress than in the case of toxic stress. In fact they may well be the cause of toxic stress, because most children feel entirely powerless in school. This is relevant to children's play, because teachers are very likely to intervene where they see normal boisterous play behavior which is actually doing no one any harm, and as we have already seen may well be doing the players a lot of good. Sadly playfulness is too often seen as a negative by teachers, who are at best overprotective and at worst obsessed with keeping order. In truth, children's apparently dangerous activity is often not dangerous at all, just mildly risky. A lot of the pushing and shoving that children do is highly choreographed, and carries hardly any risk at all. It actually primes our stress response systems, and makes us better able to cope when the risks are genuine (Sutton-Smith 2008).

The therapeutic nature of play

This brings us on to the valuable role of play as a therapeutic mechanism. Bettleheim (1988) suggested that play has a therapeutic function for the past, present, and future. Children will use play to explore unresolved problems from the past. Freud (1974) called this form of play "reconciliation." In the present a child may be able to cope either directly or symbolically with present concerns. Play may also help the child to prepare for the future by providing appropriate tools (Milteer & Ginsburg 2012; Sunderland 2008). At present play therapy and therapeutic playwork are not professions that have achieved any sort of government recognition. Yet, as we have seen in Chapter 5, the healing power of play and playwork has great potential. So, we are here making a plea for greater recognition in the official health services for the remarkable ability of play to achieve lasting change in the lives of disturbed children.

Play provision and playwork

The preceding chapter explored the potential for playwork to have an impact on the lives of all children. There has been a tendency in the UK in the past for playwork provision to be placed in areas of the greatest social and economic need. Provision should be less about compensation for social ills, and more about creating environments that enable playfulness. We would like to see the philosophy of playwork become far more widespread than the present focus on after-school clubs.

There is clearly a role for playworkers in our social institutions, from schools to hospitals to prisons. All such places could benefit from a playwork presence. So far examples of good practice are few and far between. Where such schemes have been tried they have always proved successful. However, as with most playwork provision, those projects were run on short-term budgets. That is no way to run such a valuable service. If our governments are genuine in their aim to create a better society, then we need to see more playworkers in full-time employment.

The beauty of playwork, unlike any other profession working with children, is that its starting point is the child's agenda. For that reason if no other, we should be employing playworkers, or at least adopting a playwork approach in our work with children. At present we spend large sums of money on fixed equipment playgrounds. Employing one play ranger to go out and work with disturbed and/or isolated children would be a far more cost-effective use of our money in the long run. In an adventure playground the children are constantly able to create and re-create their own play environment. That has to be better for their development, and for society as a whole, than wasting money on so-called "safety" surfacing that doesn't keep children safe.

Further reading

Brown, F. & Taylor, C. (eds) (2008) *Foundations of Playwork*. Maidenhead: Open University Press. This book contains over fifty articles focussing on a wide range of subjects of relevance to play and playwork. It presents a number of cutting-edge theoretical perspectives, interspersed with some down-to-earth examples of playwork in practice. Subjects include the play environment, the playing child, working with other professions, developing and managing play settings, children's rights and legislation, and a critique of the Playwork Principles.

Brown, S. (2009) *Play, how it shapes the brain, opens the imagination and invigorates the soul*. London: Penguin. A very thorough and well-researched book about play, which comes to the conclusion that play is as important to the human condition as breathing, and that it is crucial to the evolutionary survival of the species. Play helps brain development and is essential as a social learning tool. Brown makes a strong case for play continuing throughout life as an energizing force.

Panksepp, J. (2008). Play, ADHD, and the construction of the social brain. Should the first class each day be recess? *The American Journal of Play*, Vol.1 (1), 57–81. The young of all mammalian species benefit from ample time to play due to play's role in the construction of social brain functions. This article suggests the lack of opportunities to play in modern society may be a factor in the increased diagnosis of ADHD in children in recent times. Incidents of ADHD may be reduced if we create play sanctuaries for children where physical play is part of the daily diet of activities for all children throughout grade school.

Bibliography

ACRWC (1990) African Charter for the Rights and Welfare of the Child. OAU Doc. CAB/LEG/24.9/49 (1990), entered into force 29 November 1999.

Action Alliance for Children (2007) *Play in the early years: Key to school success. A policy brief.* Oakland, CA: Early Childhood Funders.

Adams, J., Gill, S., & McDonald, M. (1991) Reducing fear in hospital. *Nursing Times,* 87 (1), 62–4.

Adams, S., Alexander, E., Drummond, M., & Moyles, J. (2004) *Inside the foundation stage: Recreating the reception year.* London: Association of Teachers and Lecturers.

Alderson, P. (1995) *Listening to Children: Children, Ethics and Social Research.* Ilford: Barnardo's.

American Academy of Pediatrics, Council on Sports Medicine and Fitness and Council on School Health (2006) Active healthy living: Prevention of childhood obesity through increased physical activity. *Pediatrics,* 117, 1834–42.

American Academy of Pediatrics (2011) Media use by children younger than two years. *Pediatrics* 128, 1040–5, associated news release.

American Association for the Child's Right to Play (2004) *Recess news.* [Internet] Available from: <www.ipausa.org/> [Accessed 4 October 2011].

Atkinson, M. (2010) Young people contributing positively and creatively in their communities. [Internet] Available from: www.childrenscommissioner.gov.uk/content/blog/content_352 [Accessed 29 February 2012].

Augustine, S. (2001) *The confessions of St. Augustine.* Translated. New York: Signet Classic.

Ball, D. (2002) *Playgrounds—risks, benefits and choices.* Contract Research Report 426/2002. London: Health & Safety Executive. [Internet] Available from <http://eprints.mdx.ac.uk/4990/1/crr02426.pdf> [Accessed 10 October 2011].

Barros, R., Silver, E., & Stein, R. (2009) School recess and group classroom behavior. *Pediatrics,* 123, 431–6.

Bateson, G. (1955) A theory of play and fantasy. *Psychiatric Research Reports,* 2, 39–51.

Bateson, P. & Martin, P. (1999) *Design for a life.* London: Jonathan Cape.

Baxter, N. (2008) Playwork and the environment. In F. Brown, & C. Taylor (2008) *Foundations of playwork.* Maidenhead: Open University Press.

Becker, F. (1976) Children's play in multi-family housing, *Environment and Behaviour,* XIII, 545–74.

Bekoff, M. & Pierce, J. (2009) *Wild justice: The moral lives of animals.* Chicago, IL: The University of Chicago Press.

Benjamin, S. (1985) *Use of playgrounds in Leeds.* Unpublished final year project, BA (Hons.) Leisure Studies: Recreation and Environment. Leeds Polytechnic.

Bergen, D. (1998) *Play as a medium for learning and development: A handbook of theory and practice.* Portsmouth, NH: Heinemann.

Berk, L. (2004) *Infants, children, and adolescents*. Boston, MA: Allyn and Bacon.

Berk, L., Mann, T., & Ogan, A. (2006) Make-believe play: Wellspring for development of self-regulation. In D. Singer, R. Golinkoff, & K. Hirsh-Pasek (eds), *Play = learning: How play motivates and enhances children's cognitive and social-emotional growth* (74–100) New York: Oxford University Press.

Bettleheim, B. (1988) *A good enough parent; a book on child-rearing*. Vintage Books.

Bjorklund, D. (2007) *Why youth is not wasted on the young: immaturity in human development*. Oxford: Wiley-Blackwell.

—(1997) The role of immaturity in human development. *Psychological Bulletin*, 122, 153–69.

Bjorklund, D. & Green, B. (1992) The adaptive nature of cognitive immaturity. *American Psychologist*, 47, 46–54.

Bjorklund, D. & Brown, R. (1998) Physical play and cognitive development: Integrating activity, cognition, and education. *Child Development*, 69, 604–6.

Blakemore, S. & Firth, U. (2005) *The learning brain: Lessons for education*. Oxford: Wiley Blackwell.

Blatchford, P. (1998) *Social life in school*. London: Falmer.

Blatchford, P., & Sumpner, C. (1998) What do we know about break time? Results from a national survey of break time and lunch time in primary and secondary schools. *British Educational Research Journal*, 24, 79–94.

Blum, D. (2002) *Love at Goon Park: Harry Harlow and the science of affection*. Cambridge, MA: Perseus Publishing.

Bossier, E. (1994) Stress appraisals of hospitalized school-age children. *Children's Health Care*, 23, 33–49.

Bowlby, J. (1944) Forty four juvenile thieves: Their characters and home life. *International Journal of Psycho-Analysis*, 25, 19–52, 107–27.

Bredekamp, S. & Rosegrant, T. (1995) Reaching potentials through transforming curriculum, assessment, and teaching. In S. Bredekamp & T. Rosengrant (eds), *Reaching potentials: Transforming early childhood curriculum and assessment* (Vol. 2, 15–21) Washington, DC: National Association for the Education of Young Children.

Broadhead, P., Brown, F., & Waltham, S. (2011) *Research and evaluation of the Loose Parts, 'whatever you want it to be' space at Eureka!* Unpublished report for the Eureka! Children's Museum, Halifax.

Broadhead, P., Howard, J., & Wood, E. (2010) *Play and learning in educational settings*. London: Sage.

Brown, C. (2001) Therapeutic play and creative arts: Helping children cope with illness, death, and grief. In A. Armstrong-Dailey & S. Zarbock (eds) *Hospice care for children* (250–83) New York, NY: Oxford University Press.

Brown, F. (2003a) *Playwork: Theory and Practice*. Buckingham: Open University Press.

—(2003b) *An Evaluation of the Concept of Play Value and its Application to Children's Fixed Equipment Playgrounds*. Unpublished PhD thesis: Leeds Metropolitan University.

—(2003c) Compound Flexibility, The Role of Playwork in Child Development. In F. Brown (ed.) *Playwork—Theory and Practice*. Buckingham: Open University Press.

—(2007) *The Venture: a case study of an adventure playground*. Cardiff: Play Wales.

—(2008a) The fundamentals of playwork. In: F. Brown, & C. Taylor (eds) *Foundations of playwork*. Maidenhead: Open University Press.

—(2008b) The playwork principles: a critique. In: F. Brown, & C. Taylor (eds) *Foundations of playwork*. Maidenhead: Open University Press.

—(2012) The Play Behaviours of Roma Children in Transylvania. *International Journal of Play*. Vol.1 Abingdon: Taylor Francis.

Brown, F. & Webb, S. (2005) Children without play, *Journal of Education,* no.35: 139–58.

Brown, S. (2009) *Play, how it shapes the brain, opens the imagination and invigorates the soul*. London: Penguin.

Brown, S. & Lomax, J. (1969) *A pilot study of young murderers*. Hogg Foundation Annual Report. Austin, Texas.

Bruce, T. (2011) *Learning through play: for babies toddlers and young children (introduction to child care)* 2nd edn. Abingdon: Hodder Education.

Bruner, J., Caudhill, E., & Ninio, A. (2010) Language and experience. In R. Peters, (ed.) *John Dewey Reconsidered* (12–22) Abington: Routledge.

C4EO (2012) *Increasing the engagement of young people in positive activities so as to achieve the ECM outcomes*. [Internet] Available from: www.c4eo.org.uk/themes/youth/positiveactivities/ [Accessed 28 February 2012].

Castonguay, G. & Jutras, S. (2008) Children's appreciation of outdoor places in a poor neighbourhood. *Journal of Environmental Psychology* 29, 101–9.

Cavallo, D. (1981) *Muscles and morals: Organized playgrounds and urban reform, 1880–1920*. Philadelphia: University of Pennsylvania Press.

—(1979) The politics of latency: Kindergarten pedagogy, 1860–1930. In B. Finkelstein (ed.), *Regulated children/liberated children* (158–83) New York: Psychohistory Press.

Centers for Disease Control and Prevention (2000) *Promoting better health for young people through physical activity and health*. [Internet] Available from: <www.fitness.gov/betterhealth.htm> [Accessed 10 November 2011].

—(2004) *Prevalence of overweight among children and adolescents*: United States, 1999–2000.

—(2005) Preventing chronic disease through good nutrition and physical activity. [Internet] Available from: <www.cdc.gov/nccdphp/publications/factsheets/prevention/pdf/obesity.pdf> [Accessed 4 October 2011].

Charles, C. & Louv, R. (2009) Children's nature deficit: What we know and don't know. Children & Nature Network. [Internet] Available from: <www.childrenandnature.org/downloads/ CNNEvidenceoftheDeficit.pdf?> [Accessed 22 February 2012].

Children's Play Council (2002) *More than swings and roundabouts: planning for outdoor play*. London: National Children's Bureau.

Chilton, T. (2003) Adventure playgrounds in the twenty first century. In: F. Brown (ed.) *Playwork— Theory and Practice*. Buckingham: Open University Press.

Clements, R. & Jarrett, O. S. (2000) *Elementary school recess: Then and now*. National Association of Elementary School Principals, 18(4), 1–4.

Coates, G. and Bussard, E. (1974) Patterns of children's spatial behaviour in a moderate density housing development. *Man Environment Interactions,* Vol.12.

Colabianchi, N, Kinsella, A., Coulton, C. J., & Moore, S. (2009) Utilization and physical activity levels at renovated and unrenovated school playgrounds. *Preventive Medicine,* 48(2), 140–3.

Cole-Hamilton, I. (2008) Children's rights and play. In: Brown, F. & Taylor, C. (eds) *Foundations of playwork.* Maidenhead: Open University Press.

Comstock, G. & Sharrer, E. (1999) *Television: What's on, who's watchin', and what it means.* San Diego, CA: Academic Press.

Connolly, J. & Doyle, A. (1984) Relation of social fantasy play to social competence in preschoolers. Developmental Psychology, 20, 797–806.

Cradock, A., Kawachi, I., Colditz, G., Hannon, C., Melly, S., Wiecha, J., & Gortmaker, S. (2005) Playground safety and access in Boston neighborhoods. *American Journal of Preventive Medicine,* 28(4), 357–63.

Crompton, R. (1977) *Just William.* London: Book Associates.

Cuninghame, C., Hyder, T., & Kesler, D. (2001) *ECD Guidelines for emergencies: The Balkans.* London: Save the Children.

Cunningham, C. & Jones, M. (1999) The playground: a confession of failure? *Built Environment,* Vol.25, No.1. Oxford: Alexandrine Press.

Dansky, J. & Silverman, I. (1973) Effects of play on associative fluency in preschool-age children. Developmental Psychology, 9 (1), 38–43.

Darwin, C. (1859) On the origin of the species by means of natural selection, or the preservation of favoured races in the struggle for life. London: John Murray.

Davidson, G. & Barry, A. (2003) *Insight 5: Assessment of benefits and costs of out of school care.* Edinburgh: Blake Stevenson Ltd. [Internet] Available from: <www.scotland.gov.uk/Publica tions/2003/03/16823/20422> [Accessed 5 September 2011].

Davy, A. & Gallagher, J. (2006) *New Playwork: Play and care for children* 4–16. 4th edition. London: Thomson Learning.

DeLoache, J. (2002) Early development of the understanding and use of symbolic artifacts. In U. Goswami (ed.), *Blackwell handbook of childhood cognitive development* (206–26) Malden, MA: Blackwell.

Dell-Clark, C. (2003) *In sickness and in play: Children coping with chronic illness.* New Brunswick, NJ: Rutgers University Press.

Department for Education and Schools (DfES) (2007) *Early Years Foundation Stage.* London: DfES.

Dewey, J. (1916/2004) *Democracy and education.* Kila, MT: Kessinger Publishing.

Edwards, S., & Brooker, E. (2010) *Engaging play.* Maidenhead: Open University Press.

Einon, D., Morgan, M., & Kibbler, C. (1978) Brief period of socialisation and later behaviour in the rat. In: *Developmental Psychobiology.* 11, 3.

Elias, M. & Arnold, H. (2006). *The educator's guide to emotional intelligence and academic achievement: Social-Emotional learning in the classroom.* Thousand Oaks, CA: Corwin Press.

Elkind, D. (2007) *The power of play: How spontaneous, imaginative activities lead to happier, healthier children.* Massachusetts: Da Capo Press.

Ellis, M. (1987) Play and origin of species. In D. Bergen (ed.), *Play as a medium of learning and development.* Portsmouth, NH: Heinemann.

Else, P. (2009) *The value of play*. London: Continuum.

Esslemont, E. & Harrington, J. (1991) *Swings and roundabouts*. London: Save the Children Fund.

Fagen, R. (1995) Animal play, games of angels, biology, and brain. In A. Pellegrini (ed.), *The future of play theory: A multidisciplinary inquiry into the contributions of Brian Sutton-Smith*. Albany, NY: State University of New York Press.

Farrell, A. (ed.) (2005) *Ethical Research with Children*. Maidenhead: Open University Press.

Fay, J. C., Wyckoff, G. J., & Wu, C. (2001), Positive and negative selection on the human genome, *Genetics*, Vol. 158, pp. 1227–34.

Federal Trade Commission (2000) *Marketing violent entertainment to children: A review of self-regulation and industry practices in the motion picture, music recording, and electronic gaming industries*. Washington, DC: Author.

Fisher, K. (2008) Playwork in the early years: working in a parallel profession, In F. Brown, & C. Taylor (eds) *Foundations of Playwork* (174–8) Maidenhead: Open University Press.

Fjortoft, I. & Sageie, J. (2000) The natural environment as a playground for children; landscape description and analyses of a natural playscape. *Landscape and Urban Planning* 48, 83–97.

Floriani, V. & Kennedy, C. (2008) Promotion of physical activity in children. *Current Opinion in Pediatrics*, 20 (1), 90–5.

Fortunato, G. (2000) Preparing your child for urologic surgery. *Family Urology*, 1, 18–21.

Freud, S. (1920) *Beyond the pleasure principle*. New York: Norton.

—(1974) *The standard edition of the complete psychological works of Sigmund Freud*, 24 volumes, translated from the German under the general editorship of James Strachey, in collaboration with Anna Freud; assisted by Alix Strachey and Alan Tyson. London, Hogarth Press, Institute of Psycho-analysis.

Fröbel, F. (1826) *On the education of man* (Die Menschenerziehung) Keilhau/Leipzig: Wienbrach.

Fromberg, D. & Bergen, D. (2006) *Play from birth to twelve—contexts, perspectives, and meanings*. New York: Routledge.

Frost, J. (2010) *A history of children's play and play environments: Toward a contemporary child saving movement*. New York: Routledge.

Frost, J. & Kissinger, J. (1976) *The young child and the educative process*. New York: Holt, Rinehart, and Winston.

Furedi, F. (2002) *The culture of fear*. London: Fontana.

Garvey, C. (1990) *Play: the developing child*. Cambridge, MA: Harvard University Press.

Geake, J. (2009) *The brain at school: Educational neuroscience in the classroom*. Maidenhead: Open University Press.

Gibson, J. (1979) *The ecological approach to visual perception*. Boston: Houghton Mifflin.

Gill, T. (2006) Home zones in the UK: History, policy, and impact on children and youth. *Children, Youth, and Environments*, 16 (1), 90–103.

—(2007) *No fear: Growing up in a risk averse society*. London: Gulbenkian Foundation.

—(2011) *Sowing the seeds—reconnecting London's children with nature*. London Sustainable Development Commission [Internet] Available from: <www.londonsdc.org/lsdc/research.aspx> [Accessed 17 November 2011].

Gill, R. & Pratt, A. (2008) Precarity and cultural work in the social factory? Immaterial labour, precariousness, and cultural work. *Theory, Culture, & Society*, 25, 7–8.

Ginsburg, H., Cannon, J., Eisenband, J., & Pappas, S. (2005) Mathematical thinking and learning. In K. McCartney & D. Phillips (eds), *Handbook on early childhood development* (208–29) Oxford, England: Blackwell.

Ginsburg, K. (2007) The importance of play in promoting healthy child development and maintaining strong parent-child bonds. *Pediatrics*, 119, 182–91.

Gladwin, M. (2005) *Participants' perceptions of risk in play in middle childhood*. Unpublished MA Thesis. Leeds Metropolitan University.

Glover, A. (1999) The role of play in development and learning. In E. Dau (ed.) & E. Jones (consulting ed.) *Child's play: Revisiting play in early childhood settings* (5–15) Baltimore: Paul H. Brooks Publishing.

Goldschmied, E. & Jackson, S. (1994) *People under three: young children in day care*. London: Routledge.

Goouch, K. (2008) Understanding playful pedagogies, play narratives, and play spaces. *Early Years: An International Journal of Research and Development*, 28 (1), 93–102.

—(2010) Permission to play. In J. Moyles (ed.), *The excellence of play* 3rd edition. Maidenhead: Open University Press.

Gordon-Larsen, P., Nelson, M., Page, P., & Popkin, B. (2006) Inequalities in the built environment underlies key health disparities in physical activity and obesity. *Pediatrics*, 117 (2), 417–24.

Greenaway, M. (2008) Play in Wales. In: F. Brown, & C. Taylor (eds) *Foundations of Playwork*. Maidenhead: Open University Press.

Greenfield, S. (2008) Perspectives: Who are we becoming? *New Scientist*, 198 (2656), 48–9.

Grow, H., Saelens, B., Kerr, J., Durant, N., Norman, G., & Sallis, J. (2008) Where are youth active? Roles of proximity, active transport, and built environment. *Medicine and Science in Sports and Exercise*, 40 (12), 2071–9.

Haeckel, E. (1901) *The riddle of the universe at the close of the nineteenth century*, translated by Joseph McCabe. London: Watts & Co.

Hairston, C. & Oliver, W. (2007) *Domestic violence and prisoner reentry: Experiences of African American men and women*. New York: Vera Institute of Justice.

Hall, G. (1904) *Adolescence: its psychology and its relations to physiology, anthropology, sociology, sex, crime, religion and education*. Vol.1, New York: Appleton.

Harrison, P. & Beck, A. (2006) *Prisoners in 2005. U.S Department of Justice, Bureau of Justice Statistics*. Washington, DC. [Internet] Available from: <morehousemaleinitiative.com/wp-content/uploads/2008/11/doj-prison-stats2.pdf> [Accessed 7 October 2011].

Hetherington, C. (1914) *The demonstration play school*. Education, 5 (2), 697–707.

Hillman, M. (1999) Children's development in a civilised society. In: *Play Action*, Autumn 1999 (13–21) Bognor: Fair Play for Children Campaign.

Hillman, M., Adams, J., & Whitelegg, J. (1990) *One false move ... a study of children's independent mobility*. London, Policy Studies Institute.

Hirsh-Pasek, K., Golinkoff, R., Berk, L., & Singer, D. (2008) *A manifesto for playful learning in preschool: Presenting the scientific evidence*. New York: Oxford University Press.

Hirsh-Pasek, K., Golinkoff, R., Berk, L., & Singer, D. (2009) *A mandate for playful learning in preschool: Presenting the evidence.* New York: Oxford University Press.

Holme, A. and Massie, P. (1970) *Children's play: a study of needs and opportunities.* London: Michael Joseph.

Home Office (2012) *Criminal Records Bureau.* [Internet] Available from: <http://www.homeoffice.gov.uk/agencies-public-bodies/crb/> [Accessed 12 February 2012].

Howitt, D. & Cramer, D. (2007) *Introduction to Research Methods in Psychology*, 2nd edition. London: Prentice Hall.

Hughes, B. (1996) *Play environments: A question of quality.* London: PLAYLINK.

—(2000) *A dark and evil cul-de-sac: has children's play in urban Belfast been adulterated by the troubles?* Unpublished MA dissertation. Anglia Polytechnic University.

—(2001) *Evolutionary Playwork and Reflective Analytic Practice.* London: Routledge.

—(2002) *A Playworker's Taxonomy of Play Types.* 2nd edition London: PLAYLINK.

—(2003) Play Deprivation, Play Bias and Playwork Practice, in F. Brown (ed.) *Playwork—Theory and Practice.* Buckingham: Open University Press.

—(2006) *Play Types Speculations and Possibilities.* The London Centre for Playwork Education and Training.

—(2011) *Evolutionary Playwork and Reflective Analytic Practice.* 2nd edition, London: Routledge.

Hurwitz, S. (2003) To be successful: Let them play. *Childhood Education*, 79, 101–2.

ICM (2011) *Life story work.* London: Barnardo's.

Ikeda, D. (1979) *Glass children and other essays.* (B. Watson, trans.) Tokyo: Kodanska International.

James, W. (1901) *Talks to teachers on psychology: And to students on some life's ideals.* New York: Holt.

Jarrett, O. & Maxwell, D. (2000) What research says about the need for recess. In R. Clements (ed.), *Elementary school recess: Selected readings, games, and activities for teachers and parents* (12–23) Boston, MA: American Press.

Jarrett, O. (2002) *Recess in elementary school: What does the research say?* ERIC Digest. ERIC Clearinghouse on Elementary and Early Childhood Education (ERIC Document Reproduction Service No. Ed466331).

Johnson, B., Jeppson, E., & Redburn, L. (1992) *Caring for children and families: Guidelines for hospitals.* Bethesda, MD: Association for the Care of Children's Health.

Johnson, G. (1907) *Education by play and games.* Boston: Ginn.

Johnson, J., Ershler, J., & Lawton, J. (1982) *Intellective correlates of preschoolers' spontaneous play.* Journal of General Psychology, 105, 115–22.

Johnston, D. (1995) Parent-child visitation in the jail or prison. In K. Gabel & D. Johnston (eds), *Children of incarcerated parents* (135–43) New York: Lexington Books.

Jones, E. & Nimmo, J. (1994) *Emergent curriculum.* Washington, DC: National Association for the Education of Young children.

Jong, T., Gog, T., Jenks, K., Manlove, S., Hell, J., Jolles, J., Merrienboer, J., Leeuwen, T., & Boschlooo, A. (2009) *Explorations in learning and the brain: On the potential of cognitive neuroscience for educational science.* New York: Springer.

KaBOOM. (2009) *Play matters: A study of best practices to inform local policy and process in support of children's play.* Washington, DC: Author.

Kahan, D. (2008) Recess, extra-curricular activities, and active classrooms: Means for increasing elementary school students' physical activity. *Journal of Physical Education, Recreation, and Dance, 79*(2), 26–39.

Kahn, P. (2002) Children's affiliations with nature, in P. Kahn and S. Kellert (eds) *Children and Nature: Psychological, Sociocultural and Evolutionary Investigations.* London: MIT Press.

Kaminski, M., Pellino, T., & Wish, J. (2002) Play and pets: The physical and emotional impact of child life and pet therapy on hospitalized children. *Child Health Care,* 31, 321–35.

Keating, I., Fabian, H., Jordan, P., Mavers, J., & Roberts, J. (2000). Well I've not done any work today. I don't know why I came to school. Perceptions of play in the receptions class, *Educational Studies,* 26 (4), 437–54.

Keats, J. (1817) *Letter to George and Tom, 21/12/1817.* [Internet] Available from: <www.mrbauld.com/negcap.html> [Accessed 21 October 2011].

Kelvin, K. & Lauchlan, L. (2010) Thinking through transitions, pedagogy, and play from early childhood education to primary. In J. Moyles (ed.), *Thinking about play: developing a reflective approach.* Maidenhead: Open University Press.

KIDS (2010) *Playing outdoors: Disabled children's views of play pathfinders and play builder playspaces: an overview of KIDS research.* London: KIDS.

King, N. (1979). Play: The kindergarteners' perspective. *The Elementary School Journal,* 80 (2), 81–7.

Klein, M. (1932) *The psycho-analysis of children.* London: The Melanie Klein Trust.

Knight, A. (2011) *The costs and benefits of animal experiments.* Basingstoke: Palgrave Macmillan.

KOMPAN (2001) Are cities for playing in? *Leisure Manager,* Vol.19, no.5 (May) 21–2.

Krasnor, L. & Pepler, D. (1980) The study of children's play: some suggested future directions. In: Rubin, K. (ed.) *Children's play.* San Fransisco: Jossey-Bass.

Kuschner, D. (2009) From children to red hatters: Diverse images and issues of play. *Play and Culture Studies,* Vol.8. Lanham, MD: University Press of America.

La Vigne, N., Naser, R., Brooks, L., & Castro, J. (2005) Examining the effect of incarceration and in-prison family contact on prisoners' family relationships. *Journal of Contemporary Criminal Justice,* 21 (4), 314–35.

Learning and Teaching Scotland (2009) *Curriculum for Excellence.* [Internet] Available from: <www.ltscotland.org.uk/curriculumforexcellence/index.asp> [Accessed 13 October 2011].

LeBlanc, M. & Ritchie, M. (2001) A meta-analysis of play therapy outcomes. *Counseling Psychology Quarterly,* 12 (2), 149–63.

Lee, S., Burgeson, C., Fulton, J., & Spain, C. (2007) Physical education and physical activity: Results from the school health policies and programs study 2006. *Journal of School Health,* 77, 435–63.

Lees, A. (1970) Liverpool Environmental Health and Protection Department. *New Society.* 30 April 1970.

Lepore, S., Miles, H., & Levy, J. (1997) Relation of chronic and episodic stressors to psychological distress, reactivity, and health problems. *International Journal of Behavioral Medicine,* 4, 39–59.

Lester, S. & Russell, W. (2010) *Children's right to play: An examination of the importance of play in the lives of children worldwide*. Working Paper No. 57. The Hague, The Netherlands: Bernard van Leer Foundation.

Littlewood, J. & Sale, R. (1973) *Children at play*. Department of the Environment Design Bulletin 27. London: HMSO.

Locke, J. (1693) Some thoughts concerning education. In J. W. Adamson (ed.) (1922) *The educational writings of John Locke*. Cambridge, Cambridge University Press.

Ludvigsen, A., Creegan, C., & Mills, H. (2005) *Let's Play Together: Play and inclusion, Evaluation of Better Play Round Three*, Ilford: Barnardo's.

Luke, C. (1990) *Constructing the child viewer: A history of American discourse on television and children, 1950-1980*. New York, NY: Praeger.

Manwaring, B. (2006) *Children's views 2006: children's views on play and playworkers*. London: SkillsActive.

Marano, H. (2008) *A nation of wimps: The high cost of invasive parenting*. New York: Broadway.

Marcon, R. (2002) Moving up the grades: Relationship between preschool model and later school success. *Early Childhood Research and Practice*, 4 (1).

McDonald, C. (2001) Ask the doctor: Meet the professional child life specialists—making the tough times a little easier. *Exceptional Parent Magazine*, 84, 80–2.

McElwain, E. & Volling, B. (2005) Preschool children's interactions with friends and older siblings: Relationship specificity and joint contributions to problem behaviors. *Journal of Family Psychology*, 19, 486–96.

McKendrick, J. (1998) *Families and family environments in Manchester*. Occasional Paper. Manchester Statistical Society: Manchester.

—(1999a) Multi-method research. *Professional Geographer*, 51, 40–50.

—(1999b) Privatization of collective play spaces in the UK. *Built Environment* Vol.25, No.1, 44–57, special edition: Playgrounds in the Built Environment.

McKendrick, J. H. & Valentine, G. (1997) Geography matters! parental dissatisfaction with neighbourhood play provision. In: *Playlinks* April 1997, London: PLAYLINK.

McKendrick, J., Fielder, A., & Bradford, M. (2000) Enabling play or sustaining exclusion: Commercial playgrounds and disabled children. *The North West Geographer*, 3 (2), 32–49.

McKenzie, T. & Kahan, D. (2008) Physical activity, public health, and elementary schools. *Elementary School Journal*, 108 (3), 171–80.

McMahon, L. (2009) *The handbook of play therapy and therapeutic play*. 2nd edn. London: Routledge.

McMurrer, J. (2007) *Choices, changes, and challenges: Curriculum and instruction in the NCLB era. Washington, DC: Center on Educational Policy*. [Internet] Available from: <www.ecs.org/html/Document.asp?chouseid=7511> [Accessed 10 November 2011].

McWayne, C., Fantuzzo, J., & McDermott, P. (2004) Preschool competence in context: An investigation of the unique contribution of child competencies to early academic success. *Developmental Psychology*, 40, 633–45.

Medland-Fisher, S. (2011) *The play in prisons project: An evaluation. London: The Prison Advice and Care Trust*. [Internet] Available from: <www.prisonadvice.org.uk/files/Play_in_Prisons_an_Evaluation.pdf> [Accessed 26 October 2011].

Melville, S. (1999) Creating spaces for adventure. *Built Environment*, Vol.25, No.1, 71–4. Oxford, Alexandrine Press.

Mergen, B. (1995) Past play: Relics, memory, and history. In A. D. Pellegrini (ed.), *The future of play theory* (257–74) Albany, NY: SUNY Press.

Miller, E. & Almon, J. (2009) *Crisis in the kindergarten: Why children need to play in school*. College Park, MD: Alliance for Childhood.

Milteer, R., Gindsburg, K., & Mullingan, A. (2012) The Importance of Play in Promoting Healthy Child Development and Maintaining Strong Parent-Child Bond: Focus on Children in Poverty. *Pediatrics*. Vol.129.2, 204–13: American Academy of Pediatrics.

Mintel (2006) *Children's play areas—UK*. London: Mintel.

Montessori, M. (1912) *The Montessori Method*, translated by Anne Everett George. New York: Frederick A. Stokes & Company.

Moyles, J. (2010) *Thinking about play: Developing a reflective approach*. Maidenhead: Open University Press.

Mumola, C. (2000) *Incarcerated parents and their children. Washington, DC: US Department of Justice.* [Internet] Available from: <http://bjs.ojp.usdoj.gov/index.cfm?ty=pbdetail&iid=981> [Accessed 7 October 2011].

Nachmanovitch, S. (1990) *Free play: improvisation in life and art*. New York: Tarcher/Putnam.

National Association of Early Childhood Specialists in State Departments of Education. (2002) *Recess and the importance of play: A position statement on young children and recess*, [Internet] Available from: http://nccic.acf.hhs.gov/node/25324 [Accessed 10 November 2011].

National Association of Elementary School Principals (1989) National Recess Survey. Unpublished.

National Association for Sport and Physical Education (2004) *Physical activity for children: A statement of guidelines for children ages 5–12*. Reston, VA: Author. [Internet] Available from: http://www.aahperd.org/naspe/standards/nationalGuidelines/PA-Children–5–12.cfm [Accessed 11 November 2011].

NAO (2005) *Improving school attendance in Britain*. London: National Audit Office.

National Children's Bureau (2010) *Project briefing—Locked into play: Improving play opportunities for young parents in custody and their children*. London, UK: Author.

National Federation of State High School Associations (2009) *Research survey: Pay to play*. [Internet] Available from: <www.nfhs.org/content.aspx?id=3853>

National Interscholastic Athletic Administrators Association (2010) *Research survey: Pay to play*. [Internet] Available from <http://niaaa.org/>

National Scientific Council on the Developing Child (2005) *Excessive stress disrupts the architecture of the developing brain*. Working Paper No.3. Cambridge: The Council.

Newman, L. (1990) Intentional versus unintentional memory in young children: Remembering versus playing. *Journal of Experimental Child Psychology*, 50, 243–58.

Nicholson, S. (1971) How not to cheat children. the theory of loose parts. In: Landscape Architecture Quarterly. Vol.62, No.1, October 1971, 30–4—also in: *Bulletin for Environmental Education*. No.12, April 1972, London, Town & Country Planning Association.

Nicolopoulou, A., McDowell, J., & Brockmeyer, C. (2006) Narrative play and emergent literacy: Storytelling and story-acting meets journal writing. In D. Singer, R. Golinkoff, & K. Hirsh-Pasek (eds), *Play =learning: How play motivates and enhances children's cognitive and social-emotional growth* (124–44) New York: Oxford University Press.

NIfP (2011) *Play deprived life—devastating result: a tortured soul explodes.* [Internet] National Institute for Play. Available from: <www.nifplay.org/whitman.html> [Accessed 14 June 2011].

NPFA (2000) *Best play. what play provision should do for children.* London: NPFA/Children's Play Council/Playlink and Department of Culture, Media and Sport.

O'Brien, M. (2000) Children and urban space. *Childright,* October 2000, CR170

Ogden, C., Carroll, M., Curtin, L., Lamb, M., & Flegal, K. (2010) Prevalence of high body mass index in U.S. children and adolescents 2007–2008. *Journal of the American Medical Association*, 303(3), 242–9.

Ohanian, S. (2002) *What happened to recess and why are our children struggling in kindergarten?* New York: McGraw-Hill.

OnePoll (2011) *Playday opinion poll.* London: Savlon and Play England.

Opie, I. & Opie, P. (1959) *The lore and language of school children.* New York: Oxford.

Orr, D. (1994) *Earth in Mind.* Washington, DC: Island Press.

Palmer, M. (2002) *Reflections on Adventure Play (Parts 1 and 2),* London: Cornwallis Adventure Playground [video: DVD].

—(2008) The place we are meant to be: play, playwork and the natural rhythms of communities. In: F. Brown, & C. Taylor (eds) (2008) *Foundations of playwork.* Maidenhead: Open University Press.

Panksepp, J. (2002) ADHD and the neural consequences of play and joy: A framing essay. *Consciousness & Emotion*, 3 (1), 1–6.

—(2004) *Affective neuroscience: the foundations of human and animal emotions.* New York: Oxford University Press.

Panksepp, J., Burgdorf, J., Turner, C., & Gordon, N. (2003) Modeling ADHD-type arousal with unilateral frontal cortex damage in rats and beneficial effects of play therapy. Brain and Cognition, 52 (1), 97–105.

Parkinson, C. (1987) *Children's range behaviour.* Birmingham: Play Board.

Parsons, T. (1968) *Sociological theory and modern society.* New York: Free Press.

Patte, M. (2009) The state of recess in Pennsylvania elementary schools: A continuing tradition or a distant memory? In C. Dell-Clark (ed.), *Play and Culture Studies, Transactions at Play*, 9, 147–65. Lanham, MD: University Press of America.

—(2010a) The therapeutic benefits of play for hospitalized children. In E. Nwokah (ed.), *Play as engagement and communication* (3–22) Lanham, MD: United Press of America.

—(2010b) Is it still ok to play? *The Journal of Student Wellbeing*, 4 (1), 1–6.

Pellegrini, A. (2005) *Recess: Its role in education and development.* Mahwah, NJ: Lawrence Erlbaum.

Pellegrini, A. & Galda, L. (1993) Ten years after: A re-examination of the relations between symbolic play and literacy. *Reading Research Quarterly*, 28, 162–75.

Pellegrini, A. & Smith, P. (1998) Physical activity play: The nature and function of a neglected aspect of playing. *Child Development*, 69, 577–98.

Pellegrini, A., Kato, K., Blatchford, P., & Baines, E. (2002) A short-term longitudinal study of children's playground games across the first year of school: Implications for social competence and adjustment to school. *American Education Research Journal*, 39, 991–1015.

Pellis, S. & Pellis, V. (2009) *The playful brain: venturing to the limits of neuroscience*. London: Oneworld Publications.

Penn, H. (2005) *Understanding early childhood: Issues and controversies*. Maidenhead: Open University Press.

Pennsylvania School Boards Association (2010) *Special report on pay-to-play: Fees for participation in school extracurricular activities*. Mechanicsburg, PA: Author.

Perry, J. & Branum, L. (2009) "Sometimes I pounce on twigs because I'm a meat eater": supporting physically activeplay and outdoor learning. *American Journal of Play*, Fall 2009.

Pew Charitable Trusts (2008) *One in 100: Behind bars in America 2008*. Washington, DC. [Internet] Available from: <www.pewcenteronthestates.org/report_detail.aspx?id=35904> [Accessed 7 October 2011].

Piaget, J. (1962) *Play, dreams, and imagination in childhood*. NY: Norton.

Pica, R. (2005) *Reading, writing, 'rithmetic—and recess*. Available from: <www.huffingtonpost.com/rae-pica/reading-writing-rithmetic_b_877148.html> [Accessed 5 October 2011].

Pink, D. (2005) *A whole new mind: Why right-brainers will rule the future*. New York, NY: Riverhead Books.

Plato. (1955) *The Republic*. Translation and commentary by Desmond Lee. New York: Penguin Books.

Playboard (1984) *Playwork working group*. Unpublished internal paper, Birmingham: Association for Children's Play and Recreation.

Play England (2007) Charter for Children's Play. [Internet] Available from: <www.playengland.org.uk/media/71062/charter-for-childrens-play.pdf> [Accessed 12 November 2011].

—(2009) *Practice briefing 1—Developing an adventure playground*: The essential elements. London, UK: Author.

Play Wales (2011) *Play*. [Internet] Available from: <www.playwales.org.uk/landing.asp?id=3> [Accessed 2 August 2011].

Play Safety Forum (2008) *Managing risk in play provision: A position statement*. London: National Children's Bureau.

Portchmouth, J. (1969) *Creative crafts for today*. London: Studio Vista.

Postman, N. (1982) *The disappearance of childhood*. New York: Delacorte Press.

PPSG (2005) *Playwork Principles, held in trust as honest brokers for the profession by the Playwork Principles Scrutiny Group*. [Internet] Available from: <www.playwales.org.uk/page.asp?id=50> [Accessed 5 August 2011].

Pugh, G. (2004) *Sentenced families: Sign of change for children with a parent in prison*. Ipswich: Ormiston Children and Family Trust.

Pyle, R. (2002) Eden in a Vacant Lot. In: P. Kahn & S. Kellert (eds) *Children and Nature: Psychological, Sociocultural and Evolutionary Investigations*. London: MIT Press.

Ravichandran, P. & France de Bravo, B. (2010) *Young children and screen time (television, DVDs, computer)*. Washington, DC: National Research Centre for Women and Families.

Reaney, M. (1916) *The psychology of the organized game.* Cambridge: Cambridge University Press.

Riddall-Leech, S. (2009) *Heuristic play.* London: Practical Pre-School Books.

Rideout, V., Vandewater, E., & Wartella, E. (2003) *Zero to six: Electronic media in the lives of infants, toddlers, and preschoolers.* Menlo Park, CA: The Kaiser Family Foundation.

Ridgers, N., Stratton, G., Fairclough, S., & Twisk, W. Long-term effects of a playground markings and physical structures on children's recess physical activity levels. *Preventive Medicine,* 44, 393–7.

Rigg Farm (2011) *Rigg Farm Montessori Nursery.* [Internet] Available from: www.riggfarmmontessori. com/index2.html [Accessed 7 November 2011].

Rissotto, A. & Giuliani, A. (2006) Learning neighborhood environments: The loss of experience in a modern world. In: C. Spencer & M. Blades (eds) *Children and their environments: Learning, using and designing spaces* (75–90) Cambridge: Cambridge University Press.

Rivkin, M. (2001) Problem solving through outdoor play. *Early Childhood Today* 15 (7), 36–43.

Robert Wood Johnson Foundation (2007) *Recess rules: Why the undervalued playtime may be America's best investment for healthy kids and healthy schools report.* Princeton, NJ: Author. [Internet] Available from: http://www.rwjf.org/pr/product.jsp?id=20591 [Accessed 11 November 2011].

—(2009) *Active education: Physical education, physical activity, and academic performance.* San Diego, CA: Author.

Robson, S. (1993). "Best of all I like choosing time" Talking with children about play and work. *Early Childhood Development and Care,* 92, 37–51.

Rozanski, A. & Kubzansky, L. (2005) Psychologic functioning and physical health: A paradigm of flexibility. *Psychosomatic Medicine,* 67, 47–53.

Rubin, K., Fein, G., & Vanderberg, B. (1983) Play. In: P. Mussen & E. Hetherington (eds), *Handbook of Child Psychology: Socialization Personality and Social Development,* 4, 693–774. New York: Wiley.

Russ, S., Robins, D., & Christiano, B. (1999) Pretend play: Longitudinal prediction of creativity and affect in fantasy in children. *Creativity Research Journal,* 12, 129–39.

Sallis, J. & Glanz, K. (2006) *The role of built environments in physical activity, eating, and obesity in childhood.* [Internet] Available from: <www.futureofchildren.org/futureofchildren/publications/ docs/16_01_05.pdf> [Accessed 30 September 2011].

Saltz, E., Dixon, D., & Johnson, J. (1997) Training disadvantaged pre-schoolers on various fantasy activities: Effects on cognitive functioning and impulse control. *Child Development,* 48, 367–80.

Schulz, L. & Bonawitz, E. (2007) Serious fun: Preschoolers engage in more exploratory play when evidence is confounded. *Developmental Psychology,* 43, 1045–50.

Schwartzman, H. (1978) *Transformations: The anthropology of children's play.* New York: Plenum.

Sebba, R. (1991) The Landscapes of Childhood. The Reflection of Childhood's Environment in Adult Memories and in Children's Attitudes. *Environment and Behavior* Vol.23 No.4, July 1991,395–422.

Shaw, R. (1992) *Prisoners' children: What are the issues?* London: Routledge.

Sibley, B. & Etnier, J. (2003) The relationship between physical activity and cognition in children: A meta-analysis. *Journal of Pediatric Sciences,* 15, 243–56.

Sigel, I. (1987) Does hothousing rob children of their childhood? *Early Childhood Research Quarterly,* 2, 211–25.

Singer, D. & Singer, J. (2005) *Imagination and play in the electronic age*. Cambridge, MA: Harvard University Press.

Singer, D., Golinkoff, R., & Hirsh-Pasek, K. (eds) (2006) *Play = learning: How play motivates and enhances children's cognitive and social-emotional growth*. New York: Oxford University Press.

SkillsActive (2010) *Playwork People 4*. London: SkillsActive [Internet] Available from: <www.skillsactive.com/assets/0000/7086/PP4_Final.pdf> [Accessed 24 August 2011].

Slater, L. (2004) *Monkey love*. [Internet] Available from: <www.boston.com/news/globe/ideas/articles/2004/03/21/> [Accessed 19 July 2004].

Smidt, S. (2010) *Playing to learn: The role of play in the early years*. London: Routledge.

Smith, N. & Lounsbery, M. (2009) Promoting physical education: The link to academic achievement. *Journal of Physical Education, Recreation, & Dance*, 80 (1), 39–43.

Solnit, A. (1984) Preparing. In: *Psychoanalytic Study of the Child*, 7, 613–32.

Sorensen, C. Th. (1947) Personal correspondence with the author in Lady Allen of Hurtwood (1968) *Planning for Play*. London: Thames Hudson.

Spirito, A., Stark, L., & Tye, V. (1994) Stressors and coping strategies described during hospitalization by chronically ill children. *Journal of Clinical Child Psychology*, 23, 314–22.

St Co Deb (2003) *Welsh Grand Committee The Economy in Wales* col.3.

Staempfli, M. (2009) Reintroducing adventure into children's outdoor environments. In: *Environment and Behaviour* Vol.41, No.2, 268–80. Sage Publications.

Stanford University School of Medicine (2007) *Building generation play: Addressing the crisis of inactivity among America's children*. Palo Alto, CA: Author.

Stellino, M. & Sinclair, C. (2008) Intrinsically motivated, free-time physical activity: considerations for recess. *Journal of Physical Education, Recreation, and Dance*, 79 (4), 37–40.

Stevenson, H. & Lee, S. (1990) Contexts of achievement. *Monographs of the society for Research in Child Development*, 55 (1–2).

Storli, R. & Hagen, T. (2010) Affordances in outdoor environments and children's physically active play in pre-school. *European Early Childhood Education Research Journal*, Vol.18, No.4, 445–6.

Sturgess, J. (2003) As model describing play as a child-chosen activity—Is this still valid in contemporary Australia? *Australian Occupational Therapy Journal*, 50, 104–8.

Sturrock, G. (2007) Towards tenets of playwork practice. In: *IP-DiP* Issue 1, Sept–Dec 2007. Eastbourne: Meynell Games.

Sturrock, G. & Else, P. (1998) The playground as therapeutic space: playwork as healing. In: *Proceedings of the IPA/USA Triennial National Conference, Play in a Changing Society: Research, Design, Application*. June 1998, Colorado, USA.

Sunderland, M. (2006) *What every parent needs to know*. London: Dorling Kindersley.

Suomi, S. & Harlow, H. (1971) Monkeys without play. In J. S. Bruner, A. Jolly, & K. Sylva, (eds) (1976) *Play: Its role in development and evolution*. New York: Basic Books.

Sutterby, J. & Frost, J. (2002) Making playgrounds fit for children and children fit for playgrounds. *Young Children*, (57) 3, 36–41.

Sutton-Smith, B. (1982) *A history of children's play*. Auckland, NZ: New Zealand Council for education.

—(1992) *Toying with the future*. London, Channel 4 Television.

—(1997) *The ambiguity of play*. Cambridge, MA: Harvard University Press.

—(1999) Evolving a consilience of play definitions: playfully. In: S. Reifel (ed.), *Play and Culture Studies, Play Contexts Revisited*, 2, 239–56. Stamford: Ablex.

—(2008) Beyond ambiguity. In F. Brown (ed.) *Playwork—Theory and Practice*. Buckingham: Open University Press.

Tamis-Lemonda, C., Shannon, J., Cabrera, N., & Lamb, M. (2004) Fathers and mothers at play with their 2-and-3 year olds: Contributions to language and cognitive development. *Child Development*, 75, 1806–20.

Tamis-Lemonda, C., Uzgiris, I., & Bornstein, M. (2002) Play in parent-child interactions. In M. Bornstein (ed.), *Practical issues in parenting, 2nd ed. Handbook of parenting*, Vol.5. (221–42) Mahwah, NJ: Lawrence Erlbaum.

Taylor, C. (2008) Playwork and the theory of loose parts. In: F. Brown, & C. Taylor, (eds) *Foundations of Playwork*. Maidenhead: Open University Press.

Thomas, G. & Thompson, G. (2004) *A child's place: Why environment matters to children*. London: Green Alliance & Demos.

Thompson, R. (1989) Child life programs in pediatric settings. *Infants and Young Children*, 2, 75–82.

—(1995) Documenting the value of play for hospitalized children: The challenge of playing the game. *ACCH Advocate*, 2, 11–19.

Torell, G. T. (1990) *Children's conception of large-scale environments*. University of Goteborg.

Trudeau, F. & Shephard, R. (2008) Physical education, school physical activity, school sports, and academic performance. *International Journal of Behavioral Nutrition and Physical Activity*, 5(10), 1–12.

UNICEF (1991) *United Nations Convention on the Rights of the Child*. Svenska: UNICEF Kommitten.

US Department of Health and Human Services (2008) *Physical activity guidelines for Americans*. Washington, DC. Available from <www.health.gov/paguidelines/guidelines/default.aspx> [Accessed 29 September 2011].

US Department of Health and Human Services, Centers for Disease Control and Prevention. (2007) *Summary health statistics for US children: National health interview survey*. Washington, DC: US Government Printing Office.

US Superintendent of Documents (1940) *First White House Conference on Children in a Democracy*. Washington, DC.

Van Hoorn, J., Nourot, P., Scales, B., & Alward, K. (2007) *Play at the center of the curriculum* (4th edition). Upper Saddle River, NJ: Merrill/Prentice Hall.

Vygotsky, L. (1978) *Mind and society: The development of higher mental processes*. Cambridge, MA: Harvard University Press.

Waite-Stupiansky, S. & Findlay, M. (2001) The fourth R: Recess and its link to learning. *The Educational Forum*, 66, 16–25.

Ward, C. (1978) *The child in the city*. London: Architectural Press.

—(1990) Opportunities for childhoods in late twentieth century Britain. In B. Mayall (ed.) (1990) *Children's childhoods: observed and experienced*. London: Falmer Press.

Warner, C. D. (1877) *Being a boy*. New York: Houghton Mifflin.

Waters, P. (2011) Trees talk: are you listening? Nature, narrative and children's anthropocentric place-based play. *Children, Youth and Environments* 21 (1), 243–52.

Webb, S. & Brown, F. (2003) Playwork in Adversity: Working with Abandoned Children. In: F. Brown (ed.) *Playwork: Theory and Practice*. Buckingham: Open University Press.

Welsh Assembly Government (2002) *Play Policy* Cardiff, Welsh Assembly Government.

—(2008) *Framework for Children's Learning for 3-7 year-olds in Wales*. [Internet] Available from: <www.wales.gov.uk/psesub/home/framework/?lang=en> [Accessed 30 June 2011].

Wertheimer, A. (1997) *Inclusive education: a framework for change, national and international perspectives*. Bristol: Centre for Studies on Inclusive Education.

Wicklegren, I. (1993) *It's not just a game*. Current Science, 78, 4–5.

Williamson, G. R. (1985) Between home and school. Paper for *Leisure Studies Association Conference*, 1985.

Willingham, D. (2009) *Why don't students like school?* San Fransisco, CA: Jossey Bass.

Wing, L. (1995). Play is not the work of the child: Young children's perceptions of work and play. *Early Childhood Research Quarterly*, 10 (2), 223.

Winnicott, D. (1971) *Playing and Reality*. London: Tavistock/Routledge.

Wong, R. S. H. (1981) *Planning for children's play in the urban environment*. Unpublished thesis for Post Graduate Diploma in Town Planning: Leeds Polytechnic.

Wooley, H., Pattacini, L., & Somerset-Ward, A. (2009) *Children and the natural environment: experiences, influences and interventions*. Sheffield: Natural England Commissioned Report NECR026.

Wortham, S. (2006) *Early childhood curriculum: Developmental bases for learning and teaching* (4th edition). Upper Saddle River, NJ: Merrill/Prentice Hall.

Youlden, P. & Harrison, S. (2006) *The Better Play Programme 2000-2005: An evaluation*, London: Children's Play Council and Barnardo's.

Youngblade, L. & Dunn, J. (1995) Individual differences in young children's pretend play with mothers and siblings: Links to relationships and understanding of other people's feelings and beliefs. *Child Development*, 66, 1472–92.

Zygmunt-Fillwalk, E. & Bilello, T. (2005) Parents' victory in reclaiming recess for their children. *Childhood Education*, 82 (1), 19–23.

Index

0 1341 1486054 4

DATE DUE	RETURNED